BIG

TICKET

*e*COMMERCE

BIG
TICKET
*e*COMMERCE

How to Sell High-Priced Products
and Services Using the Internet

BOB REGNERUS

INNOVATION PRESS

SAN FRANCISCO

Thanks to God for His blessings,
my parents Bob and Ruth for their guidance,
my wife Arlene for just about everything,
and to my daughters Bethany and Anna
who make it all worthwhile.

About The Author

Bob Regnerus is the creator of the Big Ticket eCommerce System. He has used this system to create thousands of websites, attract more than 35 million website visitors, and generate 2.2 million leads for his clients. Bob has used the Internet to increase sales of surgery procedures, enterprise software, dentistry, rooftops, graduate programs, chiropractic treatments, and 29 other types of big-ticket products and services.

CONTENTS

Section I:
Big Ticket eCommerce

CHAPTER 1

Introduction

At the start of the dot-com boom, the media loved to hype how the Internet would change the face of business. In the media reports, everything had an "e-" added to it: e-commerce, e-sales, e-marketing, e-government, e-strategy, e-education. Internet fever was so high that a company could simply slap the letter "e" in front of its industry name and—presto!—plan its billion-dollar IPO...often in the same week! Of course, we all know how that story ended. It was "e-diculous."

Over the years, however, we've come to recognize that in e-business, the "business" part matters as much as, if not more than, the "e" part. *Big Ticket eCommerce* is written for owners and CEOs of profitable, successful, multimillion-dollar businesses—brick-and-mortar type businesses—who want to grow sales and increase profits online. This book isn't about starting up a stand-alone Internet business. It's about building on the foundation of a well-run, largely off-line business to drive Internet-enabled sales.

As such, this book describes a unique approach to eCommerce. It's an approach designed specifically to

increase the sales of high-priced products and services—
what you'll hear me describe as "big-ticket offers." Not
everything in this world can or should be crammed into
some type of online catalog tied to an electronic shopping
cart. When I remodeled my home recently, I did not
"Click here," then "Add remodeling project to shopping
cart" and "Check out." The last time I needed major
dental work, I didn't have the option of clicking on a
banner ad that promised "Buy one tooth, get the other
free." When I looked for a tax strategist for my business a
few months ago, I didn't browse an online catalog to pick
the tax bill I'd prefer to pay, and I wasn't going to get a
"Free shipping" offer if I would just "Click to buy now!"
Common sense tells us that forcing big-ticket oriented
businesses to adopt this online catalog approach to
eCommerce is, well…e-diculous.

Despite the attention given to the ever-familiar online
shopping cart, the format simply is not appropriate for
many types of businesses. But this begs the question
"What's the alternative?"

The rest of this book provides you with the answer.

Use a System That Is Based on
Real-World Experience

The system I'll describe is based on real-world
experience. My firm has created hundreds of websites for
our clients, has attracted more than 35 million visitors to
those websites, and has generated 2.2 million leads from
among those visitors. As part of this process, we've
carefully constructed nearly 100,000 online marketing

experiments to test what techniques work. It's through this disciplined process of experimentation that we have shaped the system you're about to discover.

We've used this system to enable our clients to sell a wide variety of products and services that cost between $2,000 and $2.5 million—including executive MBA programs, hearing aids, cosmetic surgery procedures, retirement plans, enterprise software, and even single-family homes. We've worked with firms in 30 industries—from Dartmouth College's Tuck School of Business to Miracle-Ear—to market their big-ticket products and services. Direct marketing luminary Dan Kennedy and North America's foremost authority on retail marketing, Bill Glazer, both recommend us to their clients that sell big-ticket items.

Pick the Right eCommerce Approach for Your Situation

As I mentioned earlier, one of the big myths accepted by many people is that there's only one way to market and sell your products and services online. Actually, there are **two** approaches.

Most people are familiar with the first approach—the eCommerce "catalog" with online shopping cart. It's an approach particularly well suited to selling products and services that are inexpensive and/or simple to understand.

If you're in the business of selling products and services that cost less than $2,000—such as books, music, clothing, airplane tickets, computers, and countless everyday items—the traditional eCommerce approach probably will work well for you.

Similarly, if you sell more expensive yet still simple-to-understand products, the traditional eCommerce approach should work just fine. An example of this would be selling spare parts for an airplane. The customer knows exactly what part number she needs to replace; she knows she can't fly safely without it. So despite the high cost, it's a simple decision-making process. In cases like this, the "Click here," "Add to shopping cart," and "Check out" process works well.

The second, almost always overlooked approach is what I call "Big Ticket eCommerce." It's designed for a specialized situation: when you happen to be selling products that are both expensive and complex.

An expensive product or service is one that costs as little as $2,000 to as much as a few million dollars. A complicated product or service is one that requires the prospect to use an extremely research-intensive decision-making process.

Often the customer doesn't even know whether he has a problem that needs to be solved; he may be quite confused about his problem and even more confused by the options available.

Products and services that fall into the "expensive **and** complicated" category include surgical procedures; multimillion-dollar software systems; industrial machinery; boats; works of art; aircraft; membership programs; and the services of dentists, attorneys, chiropractors, financial planners, CPAs, real estate agents, insurance brokers, surgeons, consultants, and general contractors.

In these cases, the prospect's buying process is a complex one. The prospect often doesn't know exactly what he wants—making the simplistic shopping cart approach inappropriate. In addition, these products and services are expensive and are typically sold without the possibility of a refund. These are big-commitment, irreversible decisions. This means the customer wants to be certain that he's making the right decision—which causes the buying process to become much more complicated.

	Simple	Complex
Expensive	Traditional eCommerce	**Big Ticket eCommerce**
Inexpensive	Traditional eCommerce	Traditional eCommerce

While the first approach may be effective for selling simple items that may or may not be expensive, as shown in the table above, the sale of expensive, complex items requires a more involved approach. In these cases, the traditional eCommerce catalog approach just doesn't make any sense. If you sell products and services that are expensive and complex, it's time to use the Big Ticket eCommerce approach.

Sell in a Way That Matches the
Way Customers Want to Buy

Most executives and owners of businesses that sell big-ticket products and services intuitively know that they need to guide their prospects toward making an informed decision. In many cases, there's a consultative aspect to this sales process—the seller assists the customer in figuring out what's appropriate for her situation, as opposed to simply taking her order. Once a prospect understands what she needs, only then will she look to buy—often from the person or company who helped her understand her situation and options.

In these businesses, the prospect's two-step approach to buying consists of (1) gathering information, and (2) choosing a specific solution for purchase. Most people can understand this commonsense approach. Irreversible, big-commitment decisions require lots of careful research. Small-commitment decisions don't.

Yet these types of "do my homework first" prospects are often frustrated when visiting company websites. Instead of finding the information that will allow them to complete their research, they are bombarded with countless "brochure websites" that implore prospects to "Buy now!" Instead of promising to educate prospects about industry basics, these websites talk only about the particular company's products and services, and why the prospect should buy them. These brochure websites blast prospects with claims that their company is better than their competitors are.

Considering that the prospect doesn't quite understand her own situation, isn't even sure she has a problem, and certainly hasn't made the decision to solve it yet—these brochure websites provide information that research-hungry prospects are *not* looking for. One of the core ideas behind the Big Ticket eCommerce system is to provide the right information to the prospect at the *right time*.

Most companies promoting big-ticket offers online get the timing completely wrong. When prospects are in "research" mode, you want to offer them educational information that helps them understand their situation and the options available to them. When prospects have chosen a solution and are in "buy" mode—then, and only then, do you want to present details about your company's specific products and services.

This timing is critical. While a low-ticket buyer can shift from research mode to buy mode within minutes and even seconds, most big-ticket buying decisions aren't impulse buys. They're carefully researched decisions that take anywhere from a few days or weeks in certain industries to months in others.

This simple principle—that you must help purchasers of high-end items to gather information before they buy—applies to financial services providers, brokers, insurance agents, accountants, and tax preparers. It works for debt counselors, Realtors, and home stagers. It's the same for dealers selling pools and spas, recreational vehicles, boats, or luxury cars. It applies to surgeons, chiropractors, attorneys, and franchise salesmen. Successful public speakers, jewelers, fitness professionals, martial arts schools, weight-loss centers, consultants, life coaches, equipment suppliers, and inventors—all of their customers rely on this two-step process for buying. When buyers use a two-step process to buy, it makes sense to match them with a two-step process for marketing and selling.

The Four-Step Big Ticket eCommerce System

Now that you understand the basics—who Big Ticket eCommerce is for and why you'd want to use it—let's dig into the details. The Big Ticket eCommerce system consists of a proven four-step approach:

1. Create the right online strategy that builds on your off-line assets.

2. Develop effective websites (usually two, not one, per company).

3. Generate appropriate traffic to your websites.

4. Analyze your performance metrics and optimize Steps 1 though 3.

At first glance, the approach seems deceptively simple. While it's easy to understand conceptually, I'll be honest: Most companies screw it up. The three biggest mistakes are:

1. Skipping steps

2. Doing steps in the wrong order

3. Executing a particular step incorrectly

Any of these three mistakes can be a fatal blow to your attempts at generating Internet-enabled sales. I encourage you to resist any temptation to decide you already understand certain aspects of the system based on the simplified descriptions above. Instead, I suggest approaching this book one chapter at a time—going through the steps of the system in the order that they are presented, as each step builds extensively on the previous one.

It's time to learn how to execute the Big Ticket eCommerce system correctly. Let's get started.

CHAPTER 2

Step 1:
Create a Strategy

Many eCommerce projects start like this: We need to be online. Let's get a website. Now that we have a website, why isn't it working better?

Let me begin by saying that a website is just a tool to help accomplish a goal—typically, the goal of increased profitable revenues. I repeat: A website is just one tool. Starting an eCommerce initiative with a website is like starting a construction project by buying a hammer. Sure, you need it, but it would be nice to develop an architectural plan first.

This is what a strategy is to an eCommerce initiative. You don't start a construction project without an architect's blueprint. Similarly, you don't start an eCommerce project without a strategy.

The Role of a Strategy

The role of Big Ticket eCommerce is to connect the prospects within your market to the products and services offered by your company. Think of a prospect who is lost and overwhelmed in a sea of choices—and suddenly a clear path emerges that leads him to a place of clarity. In this way, your strategy acts as a bridge—a bridge leading the customer down a path that ends at a purchase from your company.

If you talk to a structural engineer about how to design a physical bridge, she will tell you it starts with understanding what the bridge is intended to connect. What is the starting point of the bridge? What is the endpoint? What must the bridge accomplish to connect these two points?

The entire design of a physical bridge depends on a detailed understanding of these two points that the bridge is designed to connect. Any misunderstanding of these two points will result in the collapse of the bridge.

When it comes to Big Ticket eCommerce, your strategy is the blueprint for a "bridge" between your marketplace and your company. Similar to the architect's plan for a physical bridge, an eCommerce strategic plan depends a lot on the starting point (the marketplace) and the endpoint (your company). When you fully understand both points (and unfortunately, many companies never do), the rest of the process is about designing an effective path between the two.

The Five Elements of the
Big Ticket eCommerce Strategy

The Big Ticket eCommerce strategy consists of five important elements. Before I list them, I'll start by saying that many of these components seem deceptively simple. Don't jump to the conclusion that you have already put these elements in place.

Many of the companies that come to my firm are looking for us to bring more traffic to their website. In a lot of cases, these companies don't actually have a traffic problem (even though they think they do); nor do they have a website problem.

Often what they have is a poor strategy, or rather the lack of a well-thought-out strategy—and this is their major problem that's making it difficult or unusually expensive to attract website visitors. In other words, bad strategy often masks itself in other ways. That's why it is essential to have a solid strategy as your foundation.

Among those companies with strategy problems, most have skipped the first one or two of these five important elements. This is a lesson to companies that are seeking online success: Don't underestimate these elements or gloss over them too quickly, as that will only lead to problems down the road.

Element #1
Envisioning a Crystal-Clear Objective

What goal do you want your eCommerce project to accomplish? It seems like a simple question, but in fact, it requires some serious thought.

Let me help you break this down and think it through. Are you trying to increase sales? In answer to that question, almost everyone says yes. For what product or service are you trying to increase the sales? Most people have a specific item in mind.

The next question is, what part of the sales process is causing you the most problems? Are you easily able to get prospects to buy, but need more prospects? Do you have a ton of prospects, but experience difficulty getting them to buy? The strategy for how you handle these two situations differs significantly.

The first situation involves generating more leads from the Internet and passing those leads along using a proven off-line sales process. The second requires inventing an entirely new sales process. Depending on which situation you are dealing with, the number of websites required to get the job done differs. What you put on those websites will also differ. Either way, it is crucial to begin the process by envisioning your objective with crystal clarity. That way, you'll know you are working to accomplish your true and specific goal, and your strategy will not end up being a bridge to nowhere.

The most common scenario I see is the company that wants to generate more qualified leads from the Internet, but already has a proven sales process in place. This company doesn't want to reinvent its business. It just wants more prospects. In this case, the strategy is focused primarily on generating leads and on finding the right time and method to hand the prospect over to the proven sales system. This seems straightforward, but many clients I've worked with mistakenly try to rewrite the book. They think of their Internet project as a stand-alone silo that's separate from the rest of the business. They don't realize that they can achieve their objective using their existing strengths.

In one case, the client was refreshingly surprised when I suggested focusing the company's entire Internet effort around getting prospects to call its call center—one of the highest-performing sales call centers in its industry. This client was attempting to develop sophisticated email marketing follow-up systems—but didn't have any experience in email marketing. When I suggested that the client forget about email marketing and simply connect leads generated from the Internet to the company's proven sales call center, the client's reaction was "You can do that?"

The answer is, of course you can.

In many other client situations, I end up recommending the exact opposite. Different companies have different assets to work with and require different strategies. It all depends on your objective and on your company's specific strengths that can be used to enhance your Internet strategy.

Element #2
Reaching Prospects Online

With a clear objective in mind, you start to build a bridge from prospects in your market to the products and services provided by your company. For Internet lead generation, the first stage of building the bridge or strategy involves determining whether your target audience is actually reachable online in a cost-efficient way.

Do your prospective buyers spend time online? If so, are they using the Internet in some way that allows you to communicate with them?

For example, if your prospects frequently use search engines to learn more about topics related to your industry (home buyers are one type of online user that searches frequently), then reaching them through pay-per-click advertising on search engines or through search engine referrals can be effective.

If your prospects are online but don't actively search for topics related to your field, however, then you will need to take a different approach. For example, say your target audience consists of Realtors; they are online but aren't often searching for services related to their industry. While the typical home buyer might use a search engine to search for "Realtor," the typical Realtor does not; after all, he or she is already a Realtor. Instead, Realtors spend a lot of time on industry trade association websites and websites that publish industry statistics or news—making them reachable through these avenues.

In our examples, home buyers and Realtors are both online, but though they are related, these two audiences are reachable in different ways. If you misunderstand how to reach your audience, you'll build a bridge in the wrong place. This is why understanding whether your prospects are online and how they're reachable is essential to your strategy.

Element #3
Understanding the Psychology of the Prospect

To find the most effective way to reach the appropriate customers online, it's important to understand the psychology of your prospects. At the beginning of the strategy process, you always try to "get inside the head" of a prospect, to understand how he or she thinks. The prospect's psychological profile determines many aspects of the strategy. Let me reveal some of the questions you'll want the answers to—and why they're so important.

One question is "Is the prospect aware of his or her own problems?" If you're a dentist targeting prospects with a toothache, you'd want to know whether your prospective patient realizes she has a problem—one that can be fixed.

Next question: "Do your prospects use a common language to describe their problems?" In our example, does the person with the toothache know her problem is called a "toothache"?

When you know the answers to these two questions, you have a great deal of insight into the psychology of your prospects. It's really quite revealing. If prospects consistently use certain phrases to describe their problems, it tells you that you should use those exact same phrases in your online advertisements and your websites. You can also use certain traffic-generation techniques that work best when prospects consistently use the same vocabulary to describe their problems. You'll learn more about these techniques later.

The toothache scenario seems like a fairly obvious example, and it was chosen for that reason. Now let's look at an entirely different situation.

Let's assume you sell nutrition counseling services to people who suffer from early-stage diabetes, which can be alleviated through better nutrition. Does your prospect know he has a nutrition problem? In this case, let's say the answer is no.

Does the prospect think he has a different kind of problem? In this case, we might say "yes"—prospects think they have a medical (not a nutritional) problem. This is interesting and revealing.

Next, what words and phrases do prospects use when thinking about their "medical" problem? The answer might include terms such as "diabetes," "blood glucose monitoring," and "insulin."

The fact that the prospect exhibits consistent and predictable online behavior is helpful. It answers the question we asked in Element #2—whether or not your target audience is reachable. Figuring out what prospects are searching for, even if that search is not specifically or directly for your type of product or service, tells us how to reach them.

For example, when trying to figure out how to reach a particular audience, an important rule of thumb is to use the exact words that your prospects use. If they call their problem a "toothache," use the same word in your advertisements and on your websites. If prospects are searching for "diabetes medication," strongly consider using that same phrase—even though you sell nutrition counseling services.

But, you might ask, why not use a more straightforward approach and just advertise nutritional counseling for diabetics? There is solid reasoning behind this: You want to meet prospects on common ground—using the words they use, seeing the problem as they see it. You would never want to mention "nutrition counseling" (or any phrase the prospect isn't already using) in your advertisements or on the first website a prospect sees—the timing is wrong. You might, however, use such phrases as "alternative to insulin shots" or "how to lower your blood glucose level." These phrases speak generally about nutritional counseling for diabetics, but they use language that is consistent with the prospect's perception of the problem.

In my extensive testing, when the prospect's psychology is out of sync with the vendor's—the vendor loses. The prospect doesn't buy—especially if what you're selling is expensive.

It's easy to see why, if the psychology of the prospect is not well understood, your Internet efforts will either fail to be cost-effective—or fail altogether. This is why you must understand all the elements of strategy before you develop any type of marketing campaign or website.

You can see how a marketing campaign that focuses on nutritional counseling for diabetics would fail—it's not what prospects are interested in (at least not yet)—and any website built on that premise is likely to struggle.

You can also see how a marketing campaign that focuses on reducing blood glucose without insulin (which, incidentally, uses two key words that the prospect feels psychologically comfortable using) could deliver much better results. Websites and marketing campaigns that mirror the prospect's language and psychological biases tend to be more effective at generating leads at a lower cost.

As described earlier, this strategy builds a bridge from the prospect to your company's products and services. If you misunderstand the prospect, you end up putting one end of the bridge in the wrong place. It is difficult to make up for this miscalculation with any sort of Internet marketing tactics. An incorrectly targeted website simply will not produce the desired results.

Element #4
Identifying the Right Free Research to Offer Prospects

The next element involves figuring out the appropriate free offer to make to prospects—the offer that will get them to engage in your sales and marketing process. Here's the concept: Give prospects what they want, when they want it. Early in the buying process, big-ticket customers want research and information—not products or services to buy. If research is what prospects want, then by all means, give it to them—for free.

Why would you do this?

Let me answer this question with a story. What does every Wal-Mart buyer want before buying the physical things sold within Wal-Mart?

Answer: free and plentiful parking.

The late Sam Walton actually figured out that when the parking lot in front of a Wal-Mart is more than half full, sales inside the store drop significantly. So now all new Wal-Mart stores must meet a minimum parking lot size.

Imagine for a moment that Wal-Mart didn't offer free parking…or any parking whatsoever. What would you do if you were in charge of the Kmart or Target store across the street? If you're like me, you'd put up a big sign that says "FREE PARKING." Now all those Wal-Mart customers are going to park in your parking lot and will have to walk past your store on the way to Wal-Mart. Not every customer will walk into your store before heading over to Wal-Mart, but since customers are already in your parking lot, you get the first shot at them. It's a key advantage.

This is just one application of "giving customers what they want, when they want it."

Online, customers have no need for parking. What they do have is an enormous need to educate themselves before they make a major buying decision. Online big-ticket buyers want free and plentiful research—and they want it *before* they buy. It's their equivalent of wanting free parking before buying something in a retail store.

The difference is, Wal-Mart understands that its buyers want parking before they buy, and so the company provides it. But online, most marketers of big-ticket offers don't realize that prospects want research first, and products and services only second. These marketers are out there online, desperately advertising this product or that service, when prospects initially only want information. This creates a big opportunity for anyone who understands the "free parking" phenomenon and is willing to exploit it.

Element #4 involves identifying what kind of research to offer for free. Let's go back to our example of the diabetic nutrition counseling. Do you offer research that promises the prospect "nutritional tips for diabetics"? No, because this doesn't appeal to the prospect's current state of mind; it speaks to prospects in a language they don't yet understand. The more successful alternative? Offering free research that promises information about how to "lower blood glucose without insulin." This matches the prospect's psychological state perfectly. The fact that both promises refer to the same thing is irrelevant—the promise that mirrors the prospect's way of thinking is the only one that matters.

This free research can be packaged in a variety of ways—booklet, report, special advisory alert, buyer's guide, executive briefing, white paper, audio CD, DVD, or some other format.

Once you've determined the free research that prospects desperately want, you offer it to them for "free." While prospects don't have to pay for this free research, they do have to exchange their contact information for it. They do this typically by filling out an online request form (also known in the industry as a "lead capture form") or perhaps by calling a special telephone number set up for such requests.

Once you've generated a lead in this manner, you've accomplished several things. First, you've routed a lot of the research-hungry prospects to your company (which is equivalent to routing Wal-Mart shoppers to your parking lot). Second, your free research establishes that your company has expertise within your market and provides a "free sample" of that expertise. Finally, since you have a prospect's contact information, you can follow up consistently with the prospect, and you will have the opportunity to catch the prospect when she switches over from research mode to buy mode. When all three things happen—more leads, more trust, and more timely follow-up—you feed your sales process with a lot of highly qualified, "presold" leads.

This leads us to the last element of our strategy— where to direct a lead once we use the free guide to generate one.

Element #5
Deciding How to Hand Off the Lead

The final element of the strategy is deciding how a prospect should request the free guide that he wants. Should the prospect fill out a form on your website? Should he email your company? Should he call you?

There is not one right answer for every company. It depends a lot on the strengths and weaknesses of your own particular company.

Previously, I discussed strategy as an architectural plan for building a bridge from a prospect to your company. If understanding the prospect's psychology is the starting point of your bridge, then recognition of your company's assets and strengths is the other side of it.

For companies that are very good at inbound telesales and are generally comfortable using the telephone in sales and marketing, I recommend leading prospects to call to request the free guide. On the other hand, if your company has strong email marketing skills, I suggest having prospects fill out an online request form in exchange for delivery of the guide via email. If your company instead has solid direct-mail skills, I recommend having prospects fill out an online request form that promises to deliver the guide via direct mail.

This is where you want to take advantage of whatever sales communication medium your own organization seems to excel at using—and then link that strength to your Internet efforts.

This is where successful off-line businesses have an advantage. To exploit this advantage, you simply have to integrate your off-line assets with your online efforts—rather than thinking of your Internet efforts as a stand-alone project.

Strategy:
The Foundation of Big Ticket eCommerce

I hope you can see how important a clear and specific strategy is to the overall success of your Internet efforts. While many clients are eager to discuss improving their website content or generating more website traffic, I always have to rein them in a little in order to talk about strategy.

There is no point in building a beautiful skyscraper if it is unstable because of a problem with the foundation. In the Big Ticket eCommerce system, strategy is the foundation.

Developing a thoughtful, researched, and clear blueprint for building a bridge from the marketplace to your company is the first step. Now let's move on to the second step—picking the right kind of website.

CHAPTER 3

Step 2:
Develop Effective Websites

There is a right tool for every job. If you need to put nails into a piece of wood, you use a hammer. If you need to cut a piece of wood in half, you use a saw. If you need to create a hole in a piece of wood, you use a drill.

For most people, this is common sense. Most people don't try to cut a piece of wood in half with a drill, or use a hammer to drill a hole.

The same principle applies to your Internet website strategy. You must pick the right type of website in order to accomplish your objectives. Unfortunately, 95% of the companies I see attempting to sell big-ticket products and services use the wrong type of website.

This happens because many people are not aware of all the major types of websites available, and when each type should be used. It's like trying to build a house without ever being aware of the existence of a hammer. When you aren't aware of the right tool for the job, it's impossible to use that tool.

So let's start by defining the three types of websites. I'll follow that up by explaining who should be using each type and when they should be using it.

Website Type #1: The eCommerce Catalog Website

The traditional eCommerce catalog website is best represented by Amazon.com. This is what most business owners think of when they are building their own site. It displays a product with a brief description of features and price, and it provides an online shopping cart on which buyers can click to make their purchase.

This type of website works well to sell low-price-point products that are relatively simple to understand—books, DVDs, inkjet cartridges, coat hangers, towels, and countless other everyday items.

These are fairly straightforward products; buyers are already familiar with the category of product (everyone already knows what a coat hanger is!). The purpose of the catalog website is simply to help the buyer find the right variation of the product (e.g., color, size) for his needs and to process the transaction.

If you sell these kinds of low-price-point, easy-to-understand products, an eCommerce catalog website makes a lot of sense for you.

Website Type #2: The Brochure Website

The second type of website—one you also are familiar with—is the brochure-style or corporate website. This site contains numerous pages with lots of information about the company, including your office locations and contacts, downloadable manuals, user forums, and a Frequently Asked Questions (FAQ) page.

This type of website is excellent for serving a company's existing clients. Clients want quick and easy access to your office hours, phone numbers, address, directions, and map. They want a reminder of your various policies (scheduling, returns, canceled appointments, etc.).

This type of website is also useful for nurturing a preexisting relationship with a prospect. It's an effective way to educate and to answer the most basic questions from someone who has already heard of you, is intrigued, and wants to learn more.

The brochure website is not really useful for prospects with whom you have not yet established a relationship. It's an online resource center for the people who have *already* decided they want to learn more about your company, products, and services.

Website Type #3: The Lead Generation Website

A lead generation website is a specialized site designed to generate leads and collect contact information for prospects who may or may not be interested in your big-ticket offerings. The lead generation website is designed to serve this purpose only.

Whereas a brochure website provides resources to prospects who have already decided to learn more from your company, the lead generation website attracts and convinces early-stage prospects to *decide* to learn more about your company.

You'll learn more about lead generation websites in the next chapter, but for right now, I'll say that this style of website differs from brochure websites in several ways.

First, it's focused exclusively on information for early-stage prospects—any information that's useful for existing clients and late-stage prospects is eliminated in order to avoid distraction.

Second, the sole purpose of a lead generation website is to capture the contact information of the prospect so you can follow up with her. You will be introducing the prospect to your brochure website—but only after you've captured her contact info.

Third, the lead generation website almost never mentions, let alone sells, any products or services whatsoever. It only "sells" one thing—your free research, in exchange for the prospect's contact information.

Picking the Right Website for the Job

As you can see, these three websites differ greatly. They are suited for different situations and objectives. Step 2 of the four-step Big Ticket eCommerce system is to decide which type of website to use for your business and when to use it.

If you pick the wrong type, it doesn't matter how nice the website is—it won't be effective. It doesn't help you to have the nicest hammer on the block when the problem at hand is to drill holes in the wood.

Many companies with big-ticket products and services to offer make this grave mistake. From such a flawed foundation, it's nearly impossible to get good results.

Creating Big-Ticket Sales Often Requires Two Websites

To increase sales of big-ticket items, you often need two types of websites—a lead generation website to generate leads and a brochure website to help convince prospects to buy. The key to success with the first type is getting a prospect to stop long enough to pay attention to your company—that is, establishing an audience. The key to the latter is explaining to your audience what you have to offer and talking about the specifics of your solution.

Phrased differently, lead generation websites get people *in the door.* Brochure websites get them to buy *after* they're in the door. Each is designed for a specific purpose, and the best results come from picking the right website for each phase of your sales process.

Now let's talk about these two types of websites in more detail. You'll see the specifics behind each type—how they're different and how they complement each other.

CHAPTER 4

Attracting Big-Ticket Prospects With a Lead Generation Website

People spending a lot of money on complicated things want to be certain they are making the right decision. They do their homework before they buy.

Let me ask you a question: Should you create a website that helps your prospects do their homework, or a website that helps them buy? Which option makes the most sense? Which website is the right choice?

The Importance of Timing

The instinctive reaction of most people is to pick the website that focuses on the outcome you want—the one that sells the company's products or services. After all, it seems like the smart choice—the fastest and most efficient way to close the sale.

By this logic, however, the smart thing to do on a first date would be to propose marriage. That's the fastest and most efficient way to get the outcome you want, isn't it? But of course, this seems pretty ridiculous. Everyone knows that, whether you're a man or a woman, proposing marriage on the first date is the kiss of death. No sane person says yes to such a big commitment on the first encounter. Because of this, even if we **want** to propose marriage on the first date, we don't. We all know it's a bad idea. It'll just scare off the other person.

Yet this is precisely what most websites attempting to sell big-ticket products and services do: They ask for a big commitment on the first encounter.

Whether you're asking someone to marry you or asking someone to buy from you, trying to achieve a big commitment on the first encounter does not work well. In fact, quite the opposite: This approach scares people off.

Sell the First Date Before Proposing Marriage

In marketing, as in dating, timing is everything. There's a big difference between asking someone out for a cup of coffee and asking that person to marry you. In much the same way, there's a big difference between asking a prospect to request a free buyer's guide or other type of research from your company—and asking him to buy from your company.

Timing matters...*a lot.*

You ask for the small commitment before you ask for the big one—it's as simple as that. This rule applies whether you are making a big-ticket sale using the Internet or dating with a view to marriage.

When you use the Big Ticket eCommerce system, your lead generation website is the site that asks the prospect out on the "first date." As you'll discover later, it's your brochure website, telephone sales team, or in-person sales force that will ask for the bigger commitment down the road.

What You Never See on a Lead Generation Website

When you ask someone out for the first time, you can approach the situation in a lot of different ways. But as we've already established, there's one thing you *never* mention on a first date—marriage.

Since a lead generation website essentially performs the same function—asking your prospect for a "first date"—the same rules apply. On a lead generation website, you never mention your products, services, features, or prices. So what do you mention?

You demonstrate your credibility as an expert in your industry. You also extend an invitation to the prospect to request some helpful research—such as a buyer's guide, a white paper, or another useful educational reference—that will help the prospect understand her own situation and options.

In short, you don't sell your company's products and services. You "sell" your company's research and expertise. Remember, big-ticket buyers consume information before they are ready to consume products or services. If a prospect's idea of a successful "first date" is learning more about her options—in the case of big-ticket offers, that would mean gathering useful information about her problems and how to solve them—then in order to get a second and a third date and so on, you must provide exactly what she wants: information.

Why Most eCommerce Attempts Fail

Attempts to sell big-ticket offers typically fail when the company asks for too much of a commitment up front. If your entire website focuses on "Buy from us, and buy now!"—then you have a problem. You're asking your prospects for too much commitment, much too soon.

It's not your fault. You may have been looking to other successful companies online for role models; most of them ask for the sale immediately. The difference is that most companies, and certainly all the high-profile ones, aren't selling big-ticket products and services. They're selling low-priced offers on catalog-style websites—where asking for the sale immediately isn't perceived as too intimidating a step for the prospect.

But you can't take a square peg and try to cram it into a round hole. Don't assume that the methods used to sell simple and inexpensive items online will work for driving big-ticket sales.

The Missing Link:
The Lead Generation Website

For most big-ticket companies that wonder why their Internet sales efforts are unsuccessful, one of the key missing items is a lead generation website. Below, we'll get into the elements that make up a lead generation website. These components work to achieve the purpose of such a site, which is not to close more sales but to get more "first dates." Naturally, the more prospects you can convince to take you up on your offer of a "first date," the more who will end up making the big commitment too.

The Five Key Elements of a
Lead Generation Website

Now that you understand the role of a lead generation website and why having one is essential for big-ticket businesses, let's get into the details.

When people come across a lead generation website for the first time, they always notice that something is different about it. What makes a lead generation website unique isn't what has been added, but what has been removed.

Visit one of my lead generation websites at www.fillmyfunnel.com to see for yourself exactly what I mean.

The first thing you'll notice on a lead generation website is there are no links. The second thing you'll notice is, beyond the home page, there aren't any web pages either. It's just a one-page site with a form to fill out in order to request more information.

Why such a sparse approach?

Using automated side-by-side comparison testing tools, I've tested nearly 100,000 lead generation website layouts, designs, and text styles to determine what works the best. These test results come from real-world experiments that carefully track what real prospects do given different website designs. Let me share with you the results of my extensive scientific testing.

One of the big insights that this testing can provide is the optimal number of choices to offer to a prospect. Do you give prospects the simplest form, with just one button to click, or do you give them the choice of clicking 10 buttons? Which is more effective in getting prospects to accept your offer of free research? My testing shows that to get a website visitor to fill out a lead capture form, the optimal number of clickable buttons on your website is one—the "Submit" button on your lead capture form.

The key to generating leads (aka "first dates") on such a website is to provide enough information to interest prospects so that they will request more information, but not so much information that they become distracted by unrelated topics or decide that contacting you will not benefit them.

Following this sparse format, the typical lead generation website consists of five key elements:

1. A headline (to get the prospect's attention)

2. A demonstration of value (to prove your credibility)

3. An offer for a free buyer's guide or free research

4. A way to request this free offer (to capture a prospect's contact information)

5. Testimonials that show your offer is legitimate

Let's look at each of these elements to learn more about them and why they're useful.

Element #1:
Grab the Prospect's Attention With a
Clear, Concise Headline

Much like a newspaper headline, the headline of a lead generation website is designed to get attention. If you talk to a journalist or newspaper publisher, you'll hear that the job of the headline is to stop the reader in his tracks and get him to read the article.

The same is true for the headline on your lead generation website. The visitor is in a hurry, so you have about three to seven seconds to give him a reason to stay. If it takes any longer than that to interest him, you risk losing him.

For each of my headlines, I come up with a clear, benefit-oriented statement that demonstrates the value of the free research and the ease with which the prospect can obtain it—simply by filling out the lead capture form. In terms of formatting, I've found that large fonts in black, blue, or red perform the best. Headlines that use phrasing to which your prospects are accustomed will perform better than any phrasing your company might prefer to use.

Remember, your headline should be about your visitor and his needs, not about your own. It should not include your company's name, logo, or slogan, because the visitor does not care about those things just yet. Your headline should not brag that your company has been in business since 1992 (or some other year), because the visitor does not care about that either. It should not welcome him to your website, because he is already there. Your visitor has an extremely short attention span, so within a few seconds, he must know the answer to the question "What's in it for me?"

Element #2:
Demonstrate Your Value to the Prospect

You've gotten your prospect's attention. Now you have to fight to keep it. And how do you do that? By giving your prospect what she is looking for at this very moment: information. Remember, the prospect is still in information-gathering mode and is looking for help in understanding her own problems, so that she can consider vendors in a more informed way.

All you need to do at this stage is demonstrate your credibility and expertise—show that you are someone whose expertise is worth trusting. The key here is really to "sell" your company as one your prospects ought to pay attention to.

For example, on my own websites, I impress visitors with my credentials in the area of lead generation websites by mentioning that I have attracted 35 million visitors to my clients' websites and have used my Big Ticket eCommerce system to generate and capture the contact information for 2.2 million leads. I'll also mention that I have created hundreds of these types of specialized websites and have used scientific testing to compare nearly 100,000 different designs and layouts to find the most profitable combination.

You'll notice that when I do this, I deliberately do not discuss my company's products or services. I don't mention my firm's traffic management services, nor do I mention our lead generation website creation service. At this stage, prospects are just trying to figure out if I'm for real—if they should trust me to give them accurate and helpful information. Products and services come later. Again, timing is everything. Give the prospect what she wants, when she wants it.

Element #3:
"Sell" the Prospect a Free Guide

Instead of trying to "sell" your product right away, communicate to the visitor that you possess useful information that can help him quickly understand his problems and options. This is a tempting offer to shorten the prospect's research process by delivering—on a silver platter—all the background information he needs to know.

Again, we're not offering products or services yet. With this third element, we're only proposing to solve the prospect's research problem. Your free guide should show the prospect what he doesn't know, simplify confusing topics, introduce unusual vocabulary, and organize his vendor selection process (which, naturally, includes your company as an option).

The guide can be delivered in a variety of formats. If you are selling vacation property, for example, a free

DVD is obviously a great way to visually demonstrate the factors a prospect should consider. On the other hand, if you're selling a high-end professional service such as tax planning, a CD might be a better choice, because the prospect can easily listen to it while driving. For more technical items, a free report or white paper can effectively establish your credibility with the prospect. I've used all these formats for my own business and for my clients' too.

Element #4:
Give the Prospect a Way to Respond to the Offer

The fourth element of a lead generation website is a way for your prospects to respond to this offer of a free guide or reference. Keep in mind the two rules of thumb when deciding on the right "response device."

First, the information you request from the prospect should be appropriate for the type of guide you will be providing. For example, if you intend to use the U.S. Postal Service to mail a guide to the prospect, your request for a mailing address appears quite reasonable. If you're going to email a guide, however, then asking for full contact information doesn't seem quite right. When the amount of information requested seems significantly more than is legitimately needed to fulfill the prospect's request, prospects will be turned off. The commitment required will seem too big relative to the benefit received.

Second, the right response device varies depending on the business. There is no single right way to ask for a response. The most common response mechanism is an information request form on your website. At other times, you may want to offer a phone number instead.

Base your decision on the strengths of your business.

For example, I suggested that one client substitute a free consultation in place of the free guide. I recommended that, rather than hosting a website form, he provide a phone number for prospects to call in order to request this consultation.

In this case, the client had excellent inbound call center operations. The telephone sales force knew how to talk to prospects on the phone, educate them, and get them to buy. On the other hand, the team had no idea how to use direct mail or publish a technical guide. In this case, we decided that the free consultation was more appropriate for the business than a free guide would have been.

As part of the strategy for this client, we built the online lead generation tactic *on top* of the foundation established successfully by the company's off-line operations. There's no need to reinvent the wheel if you can simply use elements of your business that are already working well.

You never want to do something online "in a vacuum." Decisions should always be considered strategically—as part of the "big picture" surrounding your business.

Element #5:
Show the Legitimacy of Your Claims
Using Testimonials

The final element of a lead generation website is testimonials. Despite everything good you might say about yourself, your company, or your research, skeptical prospects are much more likely to believe what someone else says about you instead.

A testimonial can be a positive quote from a client or simply a statement "name dropping" a few well-known clients. For example, I mention that my clients include Dan Kennedy, America's highest-priced copywriter and author of a dozen marketing books. I also mention Dartmouth College's Tuck School of Business and Miracle-Ear—two other prestigious clients.

All of this helps to convey that what you say has worth—and that your free guide has value too.

Statistical Effectiveness Is More Important Than Image

When it comes to lead generation websites, let performance metrics be your guide. The most frequent comment I receive from people when they see effective lead generation websites for the first time is that the sites look so plain and simple. "What happened to the logo?" people ask me. "What about elegant graphical design?"

Let me share my point of view. I used to say those exact same things; I used to think that a website needed those elements in order to be successful. But I ultimately decided to try a wide variety of website formats and designs in determining how to best generate leads. Since then, we've statistically measured one type or size of font versus another, using a logo versus no logo, online video versus no video, red font versus blue font. We've tested the text that goes on the "Submit" button, and we've even tested whether to uppercase the text on the button ("SUBMIT").

In short, we've put to the test any possible idea, technique, layout, or graphic element that we think might improve lead generation effectiveness—and we've let the market tell us what works better.

My point of view is not a personal opinion, but rather is based on an enormous set of statistical tests and experiments. We let the numbers be our guide. I would suggest that you do the same. Let the numbers lead you to the right approach over time.

We'll cover more on tracking, analysis, and optimization in Step 4 of the Big Ticket eCommerce system (Chapter 13). For now, I simply want to emphasize the point that our approach to lead generation websites has been shaped by extensive market testing.

Your Lead Generation Site and Your Corporate Site Work in Tandem

If you don't have a lead generation website, you need one. It's as simple as that. If you have a corporate brochure website that you've invested a lot of time and money in, don't worry—it's still useful. In a moment, you'll see how and where a brochure-style site fits into the Big Ticket eCommerce system. For now, just realize that the commonly seen brochure website is **not** useful for lead generation, or "first dates"—but it turns out to be quite useful for "second dates."

CHAPTER 5

Enhancing the Brochure Website

A brochure website isn't the ideal type of site to use for lead generation. It gives prospects too many choices, diluting the effectiveness that comes from an exclusive focus on capturing the prospects' contact information for leads. A brochure website focuses on selling products and services—which, for the first-time prospect, is too much commitment, too quickly.

While a brochure site makes for a poor "first date," with a few improvements it can become an excellent "second date." After your lead generation website has captured a prospect's contact information, it is time to send the prospect to your brochure website. This will provide an element of instant gratification while the prospect waits for the research guide or report to arrive.

The brochure website starts the educational and sales process, but by no means does it finish the job. For example, in my business, our brochure site includes my bio, information on various services, testimonials, and articles I've written. Outsourcing elements of your Internet effort—that is, not proposing on the first date—is a big decision; it's not realistic to expect a prospect to buy immediately. However, it is realistic to begin the educational process at this point.

The rest of my sales and marketing process involves sending the prospect a free guide via the U.S. Postal Service, accompanied by both email and telephone marketing efforts. I've found the combination to be effective in my own business, and variations of this combination are useful for many of my clients.

Each element of the marketing combination contributes something unique. The lead generation website talks exclusively about the prospect's problem and about how a free guide provided by my company can help the prospect understand her situation better; this part of the process generates lead flow. My enhanced brochure website provides useful information within seconds of the prospect filling out the lead generation form. The free guide I send by mail provides the prospect with something physical—grabbing her attention and showing her that we're more than just a web page. The email marketing campaign follows up with the prospect automatically for nearly a year—trying to "catch" the prospect as she shifts from research mode to buy mode. And last but not least, the telephone sales element is geared toward prospects who know they want to buy one of my company's services but are not sure which one to get first.

While this isn't the only combination of marketing elements that can be used to sell big-ticket offerings, it is an example of what an integrated process looks like. Notice that each part of the combination plays a specific role—it's a deliberate and coordinated effort. The enhanced brochure website is the next step in this effort.

Turn Your Brochure Website Into a Virtual Salesperson

With just four enhancements, you can turn your brochure website into a virtual salesperson—especially for big-ticket offerings. These four changes are as follows:

1. Explain why your company is unique in your industry.

2. Provide educational content such as videos, audio clips, and articles.

3. Publish testimonials and proof of the credibility of your offer and your company.

4. Include free research request forms on every page.

Each of these improvements makes the typical brochure website more effective for Big Ticket eCommerce. While a lead generation website is solely focused on (and highly effective at) capturing the contact information for new leads, a corporate site that includes these four features takes a "cold" prospect and "warms" him or her up—thus speeding up the sales cycle.

Let's look at each enhancing feature: what it means, why it's useful, and why its presence on a corporate website complements a stand-alone lead generation website.

Feature #1:
Why A Prospect Should Buy From Your Company
Instead of From Any of Your Competitors

At the end of the day, prospects want to know why they should do business with you instead of buying from your competitor—or doing nothing at all. This is not an easy question to answer, because behind it lies the true but unasked question "What makes your company different and unique?"

The first important enhancement to your brochure website is to provide a concise, "big picture" answer to this question—usually just a sentence or two. For my own company, here's what we say: "We're the first Internet marketing services company to focus exclusively on increasing our clients' sales of high-priced products and services."

For many years, Federal Express's answer to this question was "When it absolutely, positively has to get there overnight." Much more than a slogan, this phrase explained when and why you should use FedEx. At the time, it was the only company offering overnight delivery services, and it continued to specialize in this arena nearly exclusively for many years.

If your company slogan also answers this tough "big picture" question, use it. But if your slogan is something like "In business since 1985," then drop the slogan from the home page. A bland statement like this does not speak to the question of your company's uniqueness in your industry. Replace it with an explanation of why someone should do business with you instead of any other company.

Feature #2:
Educational Content—
Videos, Audio Clips, and Articles

Publishing educational content on your website, such as video clips, audio recordings, and written articles, serves a number of purposes.

First, it allows you and your company to demonstrate your expertise. A prospect wonders if your company really is the best in your industry as you claim—or if you are just exaggerating like everyone else. Demonstrating your expertise is a powerful way to show that you and your company are "for real."

On the Internet, this is especially important. When you do business in person, a prospect gets to see your body language and receives other nonverbal communication. This communicates to the prospect that you and your company are trustworthy. Professional salespeople call this "building rapport."

When it comes to the Internet, though, you don't have the benefit of building rapport face-to-face. Instead, you have to take extra steps to build rapport digitally. This often starts by proving you are actually a living, breathing human being. Publishing online videos, audio clips, and articles does this effectively. In addition, publishing such content allows you to educate prospects while demonstrating your expertise.

Second, publishing educational content plays the role of answering in more detail the question posed above: why someone should do business with your company.

For example, in my articles and videos, I describe my company's philosophy of taking a strategic approach to eCommerce. We start by understanding a client's off-line sales process—how the client develops a prospect into a customer. This enables us to create an online strategy that is compatible with the rest of the business and that exploits the company's overall strengths and assets. We find that this approach benefits our clients more than if we were to treat our contribution as an Internet-only project.

Our company philosophy is not something that we mentioned in our lead generation website, since it's more information than is needed to get a prospect to request a free guide. It's also not something we'll mention on the home page of our brochure website (for that page, we stick with the shorter, more concise "We're experts in Big Ticket eCommerce" message). But in our articles, videos, and audio clips, we delve into this topic of taking a holistic and strategic—rather than a purely technical— approach to eCommerce for our clients.

The third role that publishing content plays is educating prospects about their problems. Let's go back to our example of nutritional counseling services for diabetics. For a company that provides these services, a big challenge is the prospect's misperception of his problems. In this case, the prospect perceives himself as having a medical problem—not a nutritional one.

Earlier, I mentioned that your lead generation website should not try to change the prospect's mind about the nature of his problems. It's too much to accomplish in a first encounter. But it's a topic well suited for the content you publish on your brochure website—perfect information to convey during a "second date." The link between diabetes and nutrition can be explained using an audio recording, a video, or an article. This would take the prospect one step closer to understanding how his investment in nutrition counseling will ultimately "lower blood glucose without insulin." By publishing educational content, you can provide these "missing links" in the prospect's knowledge that have so far prevented him from buying your product or service.

Publish Content That Will Anticipate and Prevent Objections. If you come from a traditional sales background, you know that you're supposed to be prepared to overcome a prospect's objections. When you publish educational content, you prevent objections before they're ever verbalized.

Think about how much more difficult this would be if you didn't include such content on your brochure website. Imagine that the nutritional counseling business opts to skip educational content on its site. Prospects who initially don't perceive themselves as having a nutrition problem will continue to feel that way. So when a salesperson from the company calls to ask for the order, naturally the prospect will say, "No, I'm not interested." After all, why would a prospect purchase a solution to a problem that he doesn't know he has?

In this example, there's a missing link in the prospect's thought process. He may not have made the mental connection between diabetes and nutrition. Treating his diabetes with medication, not nutrition, might be the most prevalent thought in his mind.

The more missing links that exist among a prospect's initial perceptions—the more he is unaware of what the information he needs to know in order to buy from you—the more necessary it becomes to publish audio clips, videos, and articles.

Publish Content That Will Educate Your Prospect About Your Unique Methods and Results. Let me show you how these first two features interrelate.

Our brochure website explains that we have doubled the online profits for most of our clients within 90 days. Rather than make the claim and leave it at that, the educational content explains the mechanism for how we achieve this.

First, we cut our clients' advertising expenses in half, usually within the first 45 days. Often, our clients are wasting half their ad budgets without even realizing it. We spot these wasteful expenditures and just cut them. While the ad budget gets slashed in half, online sales may decline by a modest 10% to 20%. This means that the client typically is more profitable immediately. But it doesn't stop there.

Over the next 45 days, we take the money that the client was wasting, and we double the client's investment in the highest-performing, but often ignored, parts of the campaign. This more than makes up for the initial 10%

to 20% drop in sales, and it often doubles the client's original sales (or other preferred performance metric) without increasing the original ad budget.

Because this pattern is a bit complicated, we mention it on our corporate site and then explain it further in our educational content. Doing so accomplishes a few things.

First, it explains how our process works, and why the results happen in the way that they do.

Second, it helps future clients to understand what to expect.

Finally, it also serves as a form of proof of our process. We don't invent a doubling of revenues out of nowhere—we actually reduce revenues first, which is a little counterintuitive until we explain our reasoning and the expected results (doubled online profits). We also explain that our track record, while very good, is not perfect: We achieve these results for nine out of 10 clients.

Now we have gained the prospect's attention by making a claim about our company's unique qualities, and we have provided information to educate the client about our methods. But what's to stop the prospect from thinking that we are just tooting our own horn?

Feature #3: Testimonials and Proof

The third way to enhance your brochure website is to include as many testimonials as you possibly can, along with any other forms of proof that your company can deliver the goods. Prospects are asking the question "Why should someone do business with your company?" This helps them believe your answer.

Testimonials from clients powerfully demonstrate your company's ability to deliver on its promises. A good testimonial is one that describes (1) a client's situation before she bought from you, (2) what the client bought from you, and (3) the results the client experienced after buying from you. This is much better than testimonials that say, "XYZ company is a great company." Those types of statements are better than nothing, but not by much.

Other forms of proof include performance comparisons, survey results, client lists, and anything else that demonstrates—in an instant—that your company can deliver. On my own corporate website, I include testimonials from dozens of clients that have doubled online profits within the first 90 days of working with my company. While our track record is pretty good, as we mentioned above, few would believe it unless we published these testimonials.

Feature #4:
Free Research Request Forms on Every Page

Remember that you will generate more leads for every 100 visits to your lead generation website than you would with 100 visits to your brochure website. But despite your best efforts to guide first-time visitors to your lead generation site, sometimes prospects find their way to your brochure site anyway. This often happens when you publish a lot of educational content there.

Internet search engines such as Google.com, Yahoo.com, and MSN.com like referring their users to your educational content. We'll discuss this traffic generation technique in more detail in a later chapter. In these cases, naturally you don't want to turn the visitors away. You still want some way to capture their contact information—turning them from an anonymous website visitor into a lead that you can contact for follow-up.

In such cases, I recommend that clients enhance their brochure websites by putting small "free research" request forms on every page of the site. You can think of these forms as miniature versions of your lead generation website, embedded within your brochure site. Include the form at the top of your website; in a left- or right-side navigation area; and/or following an article, audio clip, or video.

Why You Shouldn't Skip the Lead Generation Site

If your brochure website includes so many lead generation elements, why not skip the lead generation website altogether and simply have a lead-oriented brochure site? Because in my scientific testing, a site with fewer links and pages is *significantly* more effective at capturing the contact information of prospects than one with lots of content is. A finely tuned, heavily tested, and carefully refined lead generation website may get 20% to 50% of visitors to request your free research. For every 100 visitors to your lead generation website, that's 20 to 50 leads you can now contact and follow up with over time. On the other hand, for a corporate website with some lead generation elements built in, getting one out of every 100 visitors to request your free research is fairly typical.

In other words, a lead generation website is typically 20 times—and in some extreme cases, 50 times—more effective than a corporate website at generating leads.

Because of my extensive testing, I've concluded that your brochure website can complement your lead generation site, but it cannot replace it.

Now let's move on to the third step of the Big Ticket eCommerce system—how to generate traffic to your websites.

CHAPTER 6

Step 3:
Generating Traffic Starts
With Keyword Research

In the physical world, if customers can't find your business, does it really exist? The same question can be asked of your online presence. If customers can't find your website, does your business exist on the Internet? Answer: It doesn't.

Getting traffic to your website is the third step in the Big Ticket eCommerce system. Once you have set your strategy and created your website, now you need traffic. Developing a strategy and creating a website tend to require a substantial effort up front, but less effort on an ongoing basis. Generating traffic, on the other hand, requires significant work both up front and in an ongoing pattern.

Traffic is the double-edged sword of the Internet.

If you generate traffic effectively, your business from the Internet can soar—often much more quickly than would be possible off-line. Frequently, doubling sales from online sources requires nothing more than a wise doubling of Internet advertising investments. Doubling sales off-line, on the other hand, can require adding more staff, leasing more office space, buying more equipment, and making countless other investments.

The flip side is that if you don't know what you're doing when it comes to generating traffic, you can lose a ton of money incredibly quickly. I've seen some people lose thousands of dollars per hour by making a beginner's mistake. No matter how much money your company makes, wasting thousands will make you cringe.

Before we get into the details of generating traffic, there's an insider's secret that is important for you to understand.

The Insider's Secret to Generating More Online Traffic

One of the big secrets to successfully generating traffic online is to recognize the true strengths of the Internet— as well as its very real limitations. If you're smart, you'll base your Internet efforts on what the Internet is good at doing. If you're not careful, though, you may accidentally base your online efforts on the Internet's weaknesses— and lose a fortune in the process. Just ask the early dot-com start-up companies how they feel about this.

When you understand this concept, you'll see how it's so easy to waste money online, and you'll also appreciate what it takes to succeed.

So what, specifically, is this important insider's secret? Targeting.

The Internet is one of the most targeted advertising media available. You have the ability to target very specific audiences and to tailor what you present to them in cost-effective ways. In fact, the Internet has a greater capability for target marketing than does any other advertising medium currently available.

The great weakness of the Internet is mass marketing. It's not so much that mass marketing online doesn't work; it does. It's just that this approach is incredibly expensive. If you treat the Internet as a mass advertising medium, you will burn through a lot of money before realizing that you've made a mistake.

When you market to a targeted audience, there's very little waste in your advertising dollars. Your investment goes directly toward reaching the audience that's highly interested in what you have to offer. Because targeting is so effective, an advertiser that adopts a targeted marketing approach can afford to pay top dollar for advertising.

Take the simple example of a dentist. When a dentist advertises in a local newspaper that reaches 100,000 people, she'll be lucky if 100 readers have a toothache at the exact time they happen to notice her ad. For the dentist, the biggest advertising cost is *not* the cost in reaching the 100 prospects who *do* have a toothache. It's paying to reach the 99,900 prospects who *don't*.

Compare this scenario to online advertising. Using this medium, the same dentist can pay to reach **only** prospects who are searching on search engines for information using the term, say, "toothache." In this case, the dentist isn't wasting money on those 99,900 people who are not interested in toothaches. She's paying to reach a very specific, highly valuable audience. For this dentist, target marketing allows her to cut out all the wasted expense of paying to reach people she doesn't want to reach—enabling her to pay a significant amount to reach her targeted audience, where the money will do the most good.

Now take an example of the opposite approach—ineffective targeting. Let's say a car dealer wants to advertise online. The dealer adopts a "mass market" mind-set, thinking that everyone over the age of 18 needs a car. The car dealer also decides to pay to advertise for people searching with the term "toothache." This clearly isn't a very targeted approach. Will it work? Yes. Will it be ridiculously expensive? Absolutely.

Advertisers that don't target must compete for ad placements against those who do target. In this competition, the advertiser that doesn't target either loses the placement or significantly overpays.

Targeting Is the Key to Cost-Effective Traffic

When it comes to traffic generation, *targeting is the key to cost-effectiveness*. If you're getting both traffic and sales today but your sales aren't profitable, you're probably overpaying for traffic. Poor targeting is the primary reason why marketers overpay for online traffic.

Using medical terminology, I would say poor targeting is the single most underdiagnosed "illness" of most Internet marketing efforts. This happens because the symptoms of poor targeting often seem unrelated to targeting. Poor targeting can cause any of the following symptoms: (1) lack of traffic to your website, (2) being outbid by other advertisers, and (3) attracting visitors to your website who do not become leads. All these symptoms, and many more, can often be linked to a single problem: lack of targeting.

If you are using untargeted traffic generation strategies in your online business, I'm absolutely certain you are overpaying for traffic. Our testing of targeted versus untargeted campaigns is conclusive in this regard.

Earlier I walked you through our process and showed you how our clients typically double sales within 90 days of working with us. How do we do this in nine out of 10 attempts? In a word: targeting. All our results would be impossible to achieve without exploiting the unique targeting capabilities of the Internet. This level of targeting is not possible in any other advertising medium, including television, radio, newspapers, magazines, direct mail, or telemarketing. The ability to exploit this unique strength of the Internet is essential to cost-effective traffic generation.

Targeting is one of the most frequently overlooked and improperly executed aspects of online marketing.

Targeting = Keywords

If targeting is the key to cost-effective online lead generation, then keywords are the tool we use to "aim" for that target. When a prospect goes online, virtually everything she does leaves a digital paper trail. This paper trail is littered with "keywords"—words the prospect searched for on a search engine, the most frequently appearing words in an article the prospect read, or the words in the website addresses of the prospect's favorite sites. In a single day, literally billions of pieces of keyword data are captured all around the world.

When you want to perform online targeting, you use keywords to define who you want to reach and how. When you pick the right keywords or phrases that responsive buyers consistently use before they buy, you get better results. When you pick poorly, you lose the shirt off your back.

Utilizing keywords sounds complicated, but in the off-line world, customers and businesses use keywords every day. When a customer walks into your local grocery store and thinks to himself, "Where's the ice cream?"—he's using a keyword phrase: "ice cream." When the grocery store has an "Ice Cream" sign above an aisle, it too is using a keyword phrase. When the customer looks for ice cream and sees the "Ice Cream" sign, there's a match; the store's targeting worked, and the store gets the sale.

But now assume that instead of having a sign specifically for "Ice Cream," the grocery store has a sign that says "Frozen Goods." If the customer is taking his ice cream search literally (which is how things work on the Internet), he's going to look around, see all the signs, and say to himself, "No ice cream." Then he's going to try the grocery store down the street.

This is the essence of targeting—figuring out all the keywords that customers say to themselves, and then using those exact keywords in all of your marketing.

Companies that advertise in the Yellow Pages also use keywords, although the phone book only has a few hundred "keywords," or categories, to choose from. And for most companies, it typically makes sense to advertise under only one.

But on the Internet, there are hundreds of **millions** of keyword phrases to choose from, and you can appear under as many of them as you want. The Internet with its many targeting options has the potential to be much more targeted and effective than the phone book can ever be.

The Human Psychology Behind Keywords

Your goal in online advertising is to attract not simply visitors but prospects. Using the right keywords is both a science and an art. It's a science because some tools exist that track keyword popularity, while others track whether people who use specific keywords end up buying. It's important to know the math and statistics behind each keyword phrase.

But keyword research is also an art. What separates great keyword researchers from adequate ones is their expertise in psychological linguistics. It's the art of figuring out the psychology of a person based on the keyword phrases he or she uses online.

Adequate researchers merely think about the product or service being sold. Great ones think about the mind of the person searching for those products or services—or, even further back, for information about the problems that the products and services solve. They think about searchers' key issues and concerns, anticipating all the words that a prospect could type into an online search box. This is why understanding the prospect's psychological mind-set early on in the Big Ticket eCommerce process—and passing it along to a seasoned keyword researcher—is so important.

For example, if you're trying to attract prospects who are open to the idea of considering dental implants, obviously you would advertise under the keyword phrase "dental implants." This does makes sense—when prospective patients know what a dental implant is and are actively looking for it by name.

But what about prospects who don't realize that dental implants exist? After all, this is a relatively new dental innovation. If you're a good keyword researcher who understands the psychology of your prospects, you might start thinking of related keywords—keywords that capture the approach of a prospect who has a problem that's solvable by implants, even if she doesn't realize such a thing exists.

For example, you might consider keywords such as "missing teeth"—since a dental implant can be used to replace a missing tooth. Or you might consider "tooth extraction," based on the idea that the prospect will soon have a missing tooth in need of replacement.

If you know your product really well, you can find an entirely different angle. You will recall that dental implants are useful not just for replacing missing teeth, but for cosmetic reasons too. It might make sense to target cosmetically oriented people who are concerned about their teeth in a more broad sense—not just about a missing tooth. So terms like "cosmetic dentist," "teeth whitening," "teeth straightening," and "improve my smile" are potential keyword phrases to consider and try.

You'll notice the commonality among these keyword examples: They reflect how a potential dental patient might think, which often differs from how the dentist herself might think. A big part of successful keyword research is about forgetting what you think you know about your industry—and getting inside the heads of your prospects to consider how they think about it.

A Proven Keyword Research Process

In our company, here's how we research keywords: It starts with a brainstorming session that includes three or so members of our team, often accompanied by our clients, who write down all the keywords we can think of. The goal is to produce an initial set of high-level words and phrases that most describe our client's business, products, and customers.

Soon the list is big enough that we dump the keywords into a spreadsheet program. Our researchers study a client's brochures, catalogs, and other printed materials in order to become familiar with the business, inside and out. They study the words used on the websites and in the printed materials of both competitors and companies selling complementary products. They even use tools that allow them to evaluate hundreds or, in some cases, thousands of websites, and they pull keywords from the relevant web pages to give us ideas.

Within a short period, we will have generated 1,000 to 2,000 initial keyword phrases. We use an entirely different set of software tools to help us create synonyms (words with nearly the same meaning) and branches (words from the same word stem). For example, our master list might include the phrases "car insurance," "truck insurance," "Toyota," and "Ford." The automated software tools will create all the possible mathematical combinations, such as "Ford car insurance" and "Toyota truck insurance." Then we use our software systems to run our list against a thesaurus. Suddenly, the software sees "Ford car insurance" and adds the phrase "Ford auto insurance." We also run our list against databases of commonly misspelled words, so we'll come up with phrases like "Fordd auto insurance," among others. Soon the list will have grown to 5,000 to 10,000 keyword phrases.

Now you want to get back to the science of keyword research. When you run advertising and other traffic generation campaigns, you want to track the performance of the campaign and organize the results by segmenting according to keyword phrase.

For example, if you advertise in the Yellow Pages under "Insurance: Auto" and track how many people called from your ad, that's a good measure of the performance of your advertisement.

This is exactly what we do for *each* keyword phrase— all 5,000 to 10,000 of them. You want to know if your ad for "Ford car insurance" performed better or worse than the one for "truck insurance." You want to know if deliberately advertising with a misspelled keyword ("Fordd") is profitable or not.

In fact, you'll want to evaluate all 5,000 to 10,000 metrics…daily.

Here's why: Whenever you have a keyword list of any size—large or small—there's bound to be some waste. Many of your best guesses will be wrong. So on "Day One" of a new campaign, your approach is fairly broad and untargeted because you don't yet know which keywords attract the good prospects and which don't. But within a few days, and certainly within a few weeks, you will start receiving real and accurate market data. The key is that you have to look at the data regularly. Otherwise, your campaign is no different than an untargeted one.

It's this ongoing vetting process of eliminating the poorly performing keywords, and increasing your investment behind the high-performing keywords, that's the key to cost-effective traffic generation. Most companies never bother doing this. When this is the case, they'll easily overpay by two to three times for their traffic, or they'll receive 50% to 80% less traffic than a competitor that has the same ad budget but is willing and knows how to target.

Creating a Mini-Monopoly

At first glance, most people think it's crazy to create such large lists of keywords. Personally, I'm glad they think this, because it means that fewer people will bother to make the effort—leaving less competition for the rest of us.

The reason we go to such lengths to dig up keyword phrases is that this approach creates the opportunity to achieve a "mini-monopoly" on that keyword phrase. When you have better intelligence on your prospect, and you turn that intelligence into superior keyword research, you get more traffic for less money.

You'll typically find that the 50 "most obvious" keywords in a market are very competitive. You will definitely pay top dollar in almost all cases. But as you look at keywords 51 through 1,000 (or 1,001 through 10,000), the competition drops off rapidly. In many cases, there's little to no competition at all.

When you can accumulate hundreds upon hundreds of mini-monopolies that are largely ignored by your competition, you get high-quality traffic at a very cost-effective price. This in large part is the reason why we're often able to double sales for our clients without changing their monthly advertising investment. We simply do more homework than our clients' competitors do, and we find our client more mini-monopolies.

In fact, one of your keywords might attract only one visitor a week to start—but that visitor could be a very good buyer. If you're the only one that has done the research to figure out this keyword, you can corner the market on this type of prospect for months and often years.

Keep in mind that each monopoly is typically quite small, but when you can add together hundreds and thousands of them, the combined impact is quite significant.

As you can see, managing a successful online presence involves a lot more than just putting up a website. It requires a disciplined process of using target marketing to bring visitors to your site. Thorough keyword research is the key to accurate targeting and continually improving cost-effectiveness.

The Keyword Research "Competency Test"

Most of the readers of this book will never end up doing keyword research themselves. In all likelihood, you will assign someone on your staff or even an outside firm to do this work on your behalf.

Let me show you how to determine whether your team is doing the right kind of keyword research needed to generate traffic cost-effectively. Here are five issues to address with your in-house or outsourced marketing staff:

1. Ask your keyword researchers to describe their research process. Does it sound like the process described above?

2. Did your keyword researchers ask you or members of your team detailed "psychological profiling" questions about your prospects and customers—before even a penny was spent in trying to generate traffic for your website?

3. Does your keyword list consist of 5,000 to 10,000 keywords?

4. When you ask for a return on investment analysis of the worst-performing 1,000 keywords: (a) Do your researchers even know which keywords are performing worst? (b) Can they tell you exactly how money was spent on each keyword in the

past 90 days? and (c) Can they tell you how much revenue (or other relevant performance metrics) each keyword delivered?

5. Can your keyword researchers provide you with a list of keywords removed in the last 30 days? And when you ask why these terms were removed, can they give you a specific minimum return-on-investment threshold that the keywords failed to meet?

If you don't get a strong and immediate "yes" answer for at least four of these five questions, you're most likely overpaying for your traffic.

There's a phrase that several of my colleagues use to describe overpaying for traffic unnecessarily. It's not a particularly polite phrase to use, but it does often seem appropriate. We say that people who make this mistake are paying the "stupid tax."

Part of the problem with marketing on the Internet is that the rules of the game change constantly—literally, from month to month. What generates traffic effectively in January can become exactly the wrong thing to do by March. I've certainly paid more than my share of the "stupid tax" while trying to figure out what does and does not work.

In the chapters that follow, I outline the traffic generation methods that have worked for my clients over the longest period of time. These methods have been developed through a process of nearly 100,000 deliberate and carefully tracked "trial and error" experiments (much of it automated), intended to determine what works and what does not work online.

These chapters will show you how to avoid paying the "stupid tax" when generating targeted traffic for your websites.

CHAPTER 7

The Five Best Ways to Generate Website Traffic

The only thing that's certain about the Internet is that nothing is certain. This is a good rule to live by when it comes to online traffic generation. All the strategies I'll share with you have worked well for my clients. However, all of them, without a single exception, have undergone massive change at one or more times in the past five years.

I've learned this the hard way (that is, I paid the "stupid tax"). In one case, for my own business, I relied overly on a single, relatively exotic traffic strategy—only to have that technique's effectiveness disappear literally overnight. Nearly $1 million a year in revenues disappeared in about 24 hours. This is my personal definition of paying the "stupid tax." Don't make the same mistake by ignoring the advice of the next five chapters.

Don't Put All Your Eggs in One Basket

The best real-world advice I can give you is to avoid putting all your eggs in one basket! The rules of the game change constantly. Trust me on this one. It's just a bad idea. I have about a million reasons why I believe this to be true.

There are no guarantees that a single Internet traffic source to your site will remain effective and sustainable. So as soon as possible, you should develop multiple sources.

Virtually every traffic source that exists, or has existed in the past, has undergone dramatic changes in terms of its effectiveness and how it is used. Three examples are banner advertising, search engine optimization, and Google's AdWords.

Traffic Generation Strategies Constantly Change

Think back to about 10 years ago, when the Internet first became popular. Remember how common banner ads and pop-ups were? That's because they were effective. Like the rest of the Internet, they were new, colorful, and attention-getting, and many dot-com companies based their revenues upon them.

But soon, users began ignoring banner ads; they got tired of playing an online game of whack-a-mole with the pop-ups. In fact, many software companies began to provide tools that blocked pop-ups entirely—an option that has now become standard for many users. Companies that relied on these ads for traffic or for revenue had to make quick adjustments—or wither and die on the vine.

Then many companies began relying solely on search engine optimization—getting as many pages of their site ranked as highly as possible on search engines. It's a good strategy. But search engine optimizers became so good at manipulating search engines that the search engines fought back by constantly changing their rules for ranking sites. Overnight, a website could go from the first results page to somewhere in no-man's- land. The rules changed so fast and so often that companies depending solely on this traffic generation technique saw their traffic numbers fluctuate like a roller-coaster ride.

Google's AdWords was another traffic source that dramatically changed. Ever wonder how Google makes its billions? One way is by having advertisers appear as sponsored links on the right side of the results page following a search; each time a searcher clicks on a sponsored link, the owner of that business pays Google a small fee.

AdWords became a very popular and powerful tool because, unlike traditional advertising media, sponsors paid only for targeted, interested users. A few years ago, many marketers treated advertising on Google AdWords as a mass market advertising medium—advertising, say, dentistry services even when searchers were looking for car insurance.

But then Google became very protective of its searchers and began to ensure that its users would always see only the most relevant advertisements. Suddenly, Google began charging advertisers much more for advertising through keywords that it considered unrelated to the advertiser's website—from five or 10 cents per click on each ad to five or 10 dollars per click. For companies relying on this technique, the costs of generating traffic shot up 100 times—without any increase in sales. And it all happened literally overnight, while they were sleeping.

Many people paid the "stupid tax" on that day (those who did may remember the exact date!). I know of several people who lost seven-figure revenue streams in the blink of an eye.

Don't let this happen to you. You want to develop many sources of traffic rather than counting on just one to perform consistently. This way, even if one dies or (more typically) requires an entirely new approach, you will have other options still working for you.

The Five Best Website Traffic Strategies

The five best ways to generate traffic to your website include:

1. Online "pay-per-click" advertising

2. Permission-based email marketing

3. Internet referrals

4. Repeat visitors

5. Picking a good location

I will cover each of these methods in the next few chapters. We'll start with online "pay-per-click" advertising. It is, hands down, the fastest way to get traffic to your website while also gathering data to validate your approach—your keyword research, your free information offer, and your overall strategy.

CHAPTER 8

Traffic Strategy #1: Online "Pay-per-Click" Advertising

The first traffic strategy you should implement is online "pay-per-click" advertising. It is the fastest and most efficient way to drive prospects to your lead generation website.

Pay-per-click advertising is the online version of advertising in the classifieds of your local newspaper. From the Internet user's perspective, they are the sponsored links that typically appear on the right side of the results page after the user searches for something on Google.com, Yahoo.com, or MSN.com. From the advertiser's perspective, these "sponsored links" are also known as "pay-per-click ads."

Unlike classified ads, where you pay a flat fee to run your advertisement, with pay-per-click ads you pay a fee only when someone clicks on your ads.

Many advertisers find this simple, results-oriented approach appealing.

Google AdWords

Google controls almost 60% of the Internet search market because it is fast and reliable, and because it has taken extraordinary steps to make sure that its search results are relevant. Search results on the left side of the page—the free side—are based on the frequency and location of keywords within the web page; the length of time the web page has existed; and, most important, the number of other web pages that link to the page in question. This makes it almost impossible for anyone to manipulate the results.

Sponsored results, on the right side of the page—the classified ads I described above—are simple: a link, two lines of text, and a web address, with no distracting graphics or copy. The advertiser has only a few words to make a statement that will compel users to click on the link to its website.

Most Internet users want only the information that is relevant to them; they don't really care which side of the page they are looking on—unlike newspaper readers, who are in entirely different modes of thinking when they are in the news and the classified sections.

To appear on the right side of the results page, companies pay for what Google calls AdWords—basically, search terms users type into the Google toolbar that reflect the information they're looking for.

Originally, advertisers could get their ads shown in the best (highest) position simply by bidding the highest amount. However, ad placement now depends on two factors: how much the company pays for each keyword search term, and how relevant the company's website is to the keyword search made by the user.

You would think that the company willing to pay more would appear more prominently on Google. Often, though, the opposite is true. Typically, it's the company with the most relevant ad that Google's system favors— by showing it more prominently and by charging the advertiser less money.

This is where the "stupid tax" comes into play. If you don't use keywords to selectively target who sees your ad, the amount you pay per click can easily be 10 times higher than the amount paid by someone who is willing to target. It's a pretty steep price to pay for inexperience, don't you think?

Targeting on Google through smart keyword selection and ensuring that your website shows similar keywords is essential to cost-effective advertising with Google AdWords.

Five Reasons to Advertise With Google First

I recommend that my clients advertise initially with Google for several reasons. First, it is the world's largest and most popular search engine. Second, it's effective. Searchers use Google because it's easy, it's fast, and, most important, it produces relevant results.

A third reason to advertise with Google is that it can be set up quickly. At times, your ad could appear on results pages just 15 minutes after you set up your account. Although it can also take as long as several hours or up to a day, it's still a surprisingly fast response relative to advertising with other media.

The fourth reason to use Google AdWords is that it's easy to use. The company provides tools, directions, and an easy interface so that an end user without any experience can set up an account.

Finally, Google is the fastest way to test the four-step Big Ticket eCommerce system from end to end. It lets you see if your strategy is sound. It tests whether your website is effective and your keywords are relevant. It tells you how much traffic your ads are generating.

Most important, AdWords leads you into the fourth step of the Big Ticket eCommerce system—analysis and optimization (which we will discuss in Chapter 13)—and this is what will ultimately determine your online success.

Why You Need to Diversify Within Pay-per-Click

Once you receive your performance metrics from Google, you can use them to refine your lead generation website, trim your keyword list, and start advertising on other major search engines, such as Yahoo and MSN. Thanks to your performance statistics from Google, you know which ads worked best and which keywords brought the best prospects, and you won't have to start from scratch with these other advertising opportunities.

Despite your success with Google, it's important to also work with Yahoo and MSN. Even though they are much smaller than Google—Yahoo has 22% of the market and MSN about 10%—each serves millions of visitors each day, and each is the market leader in some markets. Moreover, working with them diversifies your traffic source so that your traffic from Google doesn't disappear if Google implements an unfavorable policy change.

Avoid Common Pay-per-Click Advertising Mistakes

There are several beginner mistakes that you want to avoid. First, you must put a spending cap on your advertising campaigns—this limits your financial risk in case you make a mistake. Some new marketers make the mistake of setting an unlimited budget—and return to the site five hours later to find that they've spent $5,000. Cap your risk, start slow, and build up gradually as you come to understand how your ads and keywords are performing.

Second, never accept the default suggestions for your ad campaigns without scrutinizing the campaign settings first. When you start a new Google campaign, the default settings and recommendations are designed to make your life more convenient while generating the most traffic. Incidentally, my colleagues and I call this the "Give Google all of your money" feature. Never accept the default settings. Always make sure that your choices are what you intended, not what Google intended. It's another instance of the notorious "stupid tax."

Third, analyze your results relentlessly in the first few days and weeks of a campaign. You will find that the real-world test results will start coming in at a very fast pace. While that's good, it's also costing you a lot of money.

The trick is to see what's working and to trim the unprofitable ads and keywords.

For campaigns designed to generate prospects for big-ticket offers, the most common metric to measure a campaign's effectiveness is the number of leads generated. All else being equal, an ad that generates more leads (that is, more visitors who request your free research guide) is considered more successful than one that generates fewer leads. This type of metric is easy to set up, and statistics can be collected automatically using a number of tools.

From time to time, we also check to make sure the leads generated also result in sales. This is typically a more time-consuming process, as many big-ticket offers are sold by telephone or in person, which makes data collection and reporting more cumbersome. Also, in many industries, the sales cycle for big-ticket offerings takes a few weeks. For these reasons, it is best to measure new campaigns initially using the number of leads generated as the key measure of success. Then we double-check to make sure those leads become buyers, once that information becomes available and can be manually collected.

Finally, the last thing to keep in mind is that new Google advertisers pay higher rates than longtime clients do. Google assumes that new and inexperienced advertisers will have less relevant ads, so it displays their ads less frequently and at higher costs. The practice doesn't seem fair, but the company is attempting to ensure that its users have a relevant search experience.

Once your site has earned Google's "trust" by being relevant (through effective keyword targeting, relevant ads, and related websites), your ads will be shown more often and your prices will be discounted. You must be willing to be patient as the experiment plays out. A number of new advertisers have been known to get nervous or throw in the towel when their initial efforts with Google don't produce the results they expected. Don't give in to that impulse!

When it comes to Internet search engines, the most experienced marketers pay less. The less experienced marketers pay more because of that annoying "stupid tax." But remember—soon you'll be one of the experienced marketers!

Next up, we look at another powerful way to drive targeted traffic to your websites—permission-based email marketing.

CHAPTER 9

Traffic Strategy #2: Permission-Based Email Marketing

Permission-based email marketing refers to sending prospects email messages that they have requested. It generally occurs when you offer website visitors something of value—typically your free research—in exchange for their email address and other contact information.

It's the equivalent of asking someone for her phone number in order to ask her out on a first date. Now you have permission to call that person, or in our case, email her.

Permission-based email marketing is my second-favorite traffic generation strategy, after pay-per-click. When used properly, it's often more effective than any other traffic generation strategy. In addition, it's cost-effective; once you have a prospect's contact information and permission in your database, you can email her for free.

It's hard to beat free *and* effective.

There's only one reason why permission-based email marketing isn't my most favorite traffic strategy. Often it's hard to build a database of prospects that you can email without relying on one of the other traffic generation strategies, such as pay-per-click. But once you have a list of prospects who have given you permission to contact them, it's a powerful and inexpensive tool.

With this type of marketing, you're able to develop an email-based relationship with your prospects. If the invitation for a first date occurs on your lead generation website, then your email marketing provides second, third, and fourth dates—essential additional opportunities to learn more about your company.

Prospects are more likely to say yes to making a big commitment and buying if you give them multiple opportunities to learn more about your company's products and services. Permission-based email marketing is an excellent way to do this.

Create an Email "House List"

The single most effective emails are those you will send to a "house list" that consists of prospects who have already indicated their interest in your products or services. These prospects have visited your lead generation website, provided their contact information to your company, and given you permission to contact them.

Clearly, these are the prospects who are most interested in what your company has to offer and are most likely to respond to whatever offers you present to them.

Don't Even Think of Spamming Your Prospects

Naturally, something as wonderful as email is abused at times. You don't want to be one of the abusers. Permission-based email works because prospects have invited you to contact them. The opposite of invited email is "spam"—unsolicited bulk emails that some companies send to large numbers of recipients. The recipients did not request this advertising and almost always do not welcome the intrusion any more than they welcome a phone call from a telemarketer during dinner.

As an advertiser, you never want to use spam in contacting your prospects because, first, you'll be on shaky legal ground—the CAN-SPAM Act of 2003 provides stiff penalties for spammers—and second, it's completely ineffective for your type of business. You offer a high-end product or service, not the trash or scams usually offered by spammers.

You want to employ marketing practices that respect your prospects and make them feel more comfortable with the idea of a big-ticket purchase from your company. That's why you should employ a double "opt-in" or email verification process, in which users who accept the offer on your lead generation website receive an automated email asking them to verify that they want to receive the offer. In addition to being a courtesy, this practice helps avoid the problem of some malicious person putting an arbitrary email address on your online request form—inadvertently causing you to send email to someone who did not request it.

Renting Email Lists

Renting email marketing lists, as with renting postal mailing lists, can be a tricky area for many marketers. While renting such lists and marketing to these "prospects" is possible and legitimate, doing so risks entering a field that is rampant with fraud—which inadvertently may lead you to violate anti-SPAM laws and guidelines.

You can gain access to two kinds of third-party email lists: those that were assembled via legitimate, permission-based practices and those that are illegitimate. Legitimate lists are often very valuable and are rarely offered for sale. It is more common for a list owner to rent out the list to advertisers for one-time use only.

The email lists you see advertised for sale—"Buy 1 million emails for $49"—are not assembled using permission-based practices. If you mail to them, the consequences can be fierce and swift. The most common consequence is for any emails sent from your company to be "blacklisted" from the major destinations on the Internet. In other words, once you cross the SPAM line (even if you did so inadvertently), 50% to 80% of your email correspondences will likely never reach their intended destination.

When it comes to renting a legitimate email list from a reputable organization, the best results are achieved by obtaining proof of endorsement from the list owner. If the people on the mailing list know and trust the owner of the list, that person's endorsement carries enormous weight. It will often increase the effectiveness of your email by five to 15 times.

Also, when you send email to a rented list, never try to sell anything directly in the email. The likelihood of making a complex, high-priced sale with a one-time mailing to "cold" prospects is very low. The more cost-effective approach is to extend some type of free offer to the people on the mailing list—a free guide, report, audio clip, or video. To obtain the free item, then, prospects must click on a link that leads them to...yes, you guessed it—your lead generation website. Once they request the free guide and opt in to your permission-based house list, you can follow up with them over time, building digital rapport, and ultimately leading them to buy from you.

Use Automated Email Marketing Sequences

Once a prospect has opted in to your house list—and verified his desire to do so—you should immediately send him an email that confirms his request and informs him of what to expect next. Follow this with a prearranged email sequence that is common to every new prospect.

There is no preset sequence that makes sense for every business. Your sequence can include 10 emails or 40, and it can be designed to send emails at whatever intervals you determine.

But there are certain guidelines to follow. If you're sending a series of emails that build upon one another, you shouldn't spread the series out too long, because prospects may forget your previous communications.

For instance, if prospects have responded to your lead generation website's offer for a free DVD, you should email them an initial acknowledgement of the request, then automatically send another email two days later informing them that their package has been shipped.

You may wish to design your automated sequence to email prospects with useful information that will whet their appetite for the DVD while they wait for it to arrive. Then, about a week after prospects have responded to the offer, your system could email them asking them to contact your office if they have questions about the DVD.

Afterward, you can continue to email these prospects, at no cost to you, until they opt out or change their email address. Otherwise, don't stop emailing them…ever. You incurred all your expenses and effort at the start of the process, and now it costs you nothing to maintain the relationship digitally and to sustain the potential of closing more sales.

Keep in mind, you and your staff aren't manually sending out these emails one at a time. You're setting up a prewritten series of emails that will be sent out automatically, on a preset schedule that is triggered when a prospect joins your mailing list.

If one prospect joins on January 1, she receives the "Day Zero" message on January 1. If another prospect joins your list on March 31, she receives the same "Day Zero" email on March 31. For each prospect, the entire experience seems tailored to her—even though you or a staff member created the entire sequence months or even years ago.

I have had prospects on my company's permission-based email marketing list since 1999. I've continued to include these prospects in my email campaigns—keeping them informed about my company for years. It costs me next to nothing to send the exact same message to a few more email addresses. Surprisingly (even to me), a few have actually become big-ticket buyers after nearly a decade of receiving my emails! As I said earlier, it's hard to beat effective *and* free.

Now you know why I like permission-based email so much. Keep in mind that I did invest advertising dollars in 1999 to get those prospects onto my permission-based email marketing lists, but I've been marketing to those prospects (and more recent ones, of course) for the better part of a decade—for free.

Surprise Your Prospects With Time-Sensitive Broadcast Emails

The trick to using automated email marketing sequences is to create emails that are timeless. If you sent out a free guide to the prospect on Tuesday, your email a week later can say, "I just wanted to make sure you received the free guide I sent out a week ago."

Avoid any mention of specific months, dates, holidays, or seasons. That way, all the emails can work as well now as they work 10 years from now.

However, to mix things up a bit, you also want to send one-time-only, time-sensitive emails. These can be about seasonal promotions, where there's a sense of urgency to the offer, or they can be your commentary on controversial industry news that prospects are talking about.

Broadcast emails are especially useful for staying in touch with prospects who have reached the end of your predesigned email sequence but have never opted out of your email marketing list.

Unlike many other communication media, email is a "push" medium. You don't have to wait for prospects to visit your website. Instead, you "push" the information out to them. Or you can give them just a little information in your emails, and refer them back to your website for more information.

To Sell More, Give More

There's one temptation about email marketing that you need to avoid. This is the temptation to send sales solicitations to your prospects daily until they buy. After all, the thinking is, email is free.

You have to be careful with this thinking. It's the equivalent of asking someone to marry you on the second date, the third date, and so on, and intending to continue asking until that person says yes. When you do this, the only thing you accomplish is the alienation of the other person, until he or she learns to ignore you.

If the only reason you send an email is to ask for money, prospects quickly realize this and tune you out. Instead, to sell more, give more. Give out some free information that the prospect will find useful or informative. Provide news updates on your industry.

Train your prospects to realize that when you send them an email, it's an email worth reading.

When you do this, you build rapport with your prospects. They come to trust you and even look forward to your emails. From time to time, when you make your products and services available via email, your prospects will genuinely consider it.

In the dating world, you might call this "courtship." If you want someone to make a big commitment to your company, a little courtship (in this case, via email) can go a long way.

Incidentally, permission-based email marketing is one area where small companies can often outperform the big corporations. Big corporations send either hard pitches, advertisements, or very cold, industrial-type emails. It's often easier to say yes to someone you know and trust than to some nameless, faceless institution. As with courtship, a little personality in your emails goes a long way.

Use Email Marketing Automation Services

Paying a staff member to sort through email sign-up and unsubscribe requests would cost a small fortune—a successful website will have tens of thousands of email addresses to manage, with a certain percentage of those addresses changing or unsubscribing each month.

To make this process cost-effective, you must automate it with an automatic responder software system that manages the process for you. These programs send emails based on a prearranged, coded sequence.

Auto responder programs never ask for a commission, never call in sick, and never forget to send an email on time. A good one will even personalize your messages, so that recipients see their own name at the top of the email—often leading them to believe that you sent it personally. This personal touch increases your response rate.

You can prepare emails that answer anticipated questions or objections. This educates and pre-sells prospects on your products and services. Auto responders also enable you to send one email sequence to established customers and a different one to prospects. They allow you to create customized sequences for prospects interested in each type of product or service. They enable you to maintain contact with customers so they become, or remain, repeat customers.

I highly recommend that you use a high-quality auto-responder software service to manage your email marketing efforts. First, it will do all the things that you require in order to be successful, such as personalizing your message and including an unsubscribe link, which is required by law.

Second, you will have much more success making sure your messages actually get delivered to their intended recipients. If you try to use your own email account, or if you use a substandard auto responder, there is a good chance that one of the major service providers, such as Yahoo or AOL, will flag your message as spam. Half of your recipients might not even receive the email you sent, and you would never even know it.

A decent auto-responder service has a good reputation with the major service providers and has far less trouble getting your messages through. Remember, an email is completely ineffective if the intended recipient never receives it.

To see what an auto responder sequence looks like, visit my brochure website at www.theleadsking.com. You'll see a miniature free resources request form. Fill it out, and you'll automatically receive a series of email messages with information on how to get more traffic to your website. You will receive a dozen or more emails that provide useful information over a period of a few weeks. This will give you a good idea of how an auto responder schedules and personalizes its messages.

CHAPTER 10

Traffic Strategy #3:
Internet Referrals

In your off-line business, you know referrals are an important source for generating high-quality leads. People have faith in products and services recommended to them by people they already trust.

If your three best friends tell you to see a new movie, you're much more likely to go than if they had not recommended it.

The same idea works online. Only, instead of other people recommending your company to prospects, it's other websites. It's not only your prospects who notice these referrals, but also the major search engines, such as Google and Yahoo.

You'll often hear jargon used, like "search engine optimization" (or "SEO" for short), "organic search," "search engine marketing," or "free traffic." All these terms refer to the time-tested method of getting new business through referrals.

Links = Referrals

Links from other websites are the most important criteria that Google and other search engines use to determine your site's ranking among the search engine's free search results. Each link from a third-party website to your website is considered a referral, and is a vote that your company's website is useful and relevant. While you can still pay for your pay-per-click ads to appear prominently on search result pages, your ads can also appear there for free, if other websites "vote" (by linking to your website) that your website is a good one.

In the off-line world, getting an endorsement from your neighbor is not the same as being endorsed by an authority figure, such as Oprah on her television show. In the world of off-line referrals, the reputation of the person making the referral matters a lot.

The same is true online. A link from a prominent website such as CNN.com or Yahoo.com is more influential than a link from your neighbor's personal website. Instead of authority figures, these prominent websites—such as CNN and Yahoo—are known as "authority websites."

Of course, websites like CNN and Yahoo are the most influential and most authoritative websites on the Internet. There are also a number of mid-level authority sites that are worth getting links and referrals from.

Google has an authority rating scale that measures the authority level of a particular website or web page. It's a 10-point scale called "PageRank." A brand-new website (like your neighbor's personal web page) most likely has a

0 rating. Google's home page has a 10 rating. The home pages of NYTimes.com, CNN.com, and Yahoo.com all have 9 ratings.

To put things in perspective, for most people reading this book, getting a handful of links and referrals from mid-level authority sites with a 4 or 5 rating would cause a noticeable increase in traffic and sales.

When you get a link from an authority website, two things happen. First, people see the link on the authority website, click the link, and end up on your website. Second, search engines like Google notice these endorsements, and improve the prominence of your free listings in their search engine. Algorithms like Google's are based on the idea that if CNN.com says your website is important and newsworthy, it must be true. It's similar to the idea that if Oprah endorses something, it must be good. In both these cases, the influence of the endorsement is less about your website and more about the reputation of the endorser.

Both the direct traffic from authority websites and the increased prominence on search engines (which also refers search engine users to your website) end up driving more traffic to your website.

Four Ways to Get Referrals (aka "Links") From Authority Websites

In the physical world, you build your business reputation by networking in your community, speaking at industry events, and being quoted by industry publications. The process online is similar. You want to appear prominently in influential places online—and in turn, get links back to your website.

There are four ways to do this. Let's look at each method.

1) Publish Useful Content on Your Website

The first method for getting links from authority sites (and in the process, increasing your website's ranking on free search engine listings) is to publish genuinely useful and informative content on your website. When you publish useful content, the people who produce content on authority websites notice it and link to it naturally, as a way to refer their visitors to interesting resources online.

Here's an old example that illustrates the point. Several years ago, some of the early mortgage websites on the Internet published daily mortgage rate updates on their websites. At the time, none of their competitors were doing this. All the authority websites in the personal finance arena linked to these sites—generating free referral traffic for these innovative mortgage websites.

As the Internet matured, and every mortgage company began to publish its rates online, the more innovative sites started providing personalized mortgage rate calculators. Instead of seeing just the average market rate for a mortgage, you could enter your personal profile and credit scores to receive your *personal* mortgage rate. At the time, this was so useful and unique that all the personal finance authority sites linked to these websites all over again.

While the mortgage arena is an exceptionally competitive multibillion-dollar market online, publishing a bunch of useful "how to" articles about your industry is more than enough to get things started in most markets. Instead of a single FAQ web page, publish an entire article for each frequently asked question. This content is a natural fit for your brochure website.

While my strong preference is to encourage prospects to visit your lead generation website first, this is the one exception to that rule. When you use the "publish content" approach to generating free traffic, and you do it well, the results can be quite positive. While a lead generation website is more effective than a corporate website at capturing a prospect's contact information (in some cases, 10 to 50 times more effective), a corporate website with a lot of content can get more "free" traffic than a lead generation website can provide.

So which approach is best? Personally, I use all the methods I've mentioned so far to generate traffic. However, I do strongly prefer starting with the combination of pay-per-click advertising and a lead generation website. Following this order will allow the market insight and testing of keywords to show you what free content to publish on your brochure website.

For example, a number of my new clients have had brochure websites with a lot of content. Yet these sites may not receive any free traffic or obtain any links from authority sites. After a little research, it turns out that these clients have a lot of wrong content on their brochure website.

Just as all referrals are not created equally, all content is not created equally either. I'll discuss this in more detail after covering the remaining three ways to generate referrals.

2) Syndicate Content Through Syndication Services

The second method involves a technique called "content syndication." The simplest example of content syndication is to look in your local newspaper. Look at the comic strip section or the Dear Abby column; those are examples of syndicated content. Your favorite comic strip actually appears in hundreds of newspapers around the country. So does the Dear Abby column. The content is created by the comic strip artist or columnist, and is syndicated to multiple publications.

Most of the syndicated content you see in newspapers is provided by "content middlemen" or syndication services. The content creator has a single point of contact, the syndication service, that deals with getting the comic strip or column distributed to hundreds of publications before each publication's deadline.

Something similar takes place online. Content middlemen, or online content syndication services, have also appeared over the past few years. You publish your articles or columns with these services, and the services distribute your content to websites eager to republish it.

It's a simple model that's quite effective at getting your content widely distributed.

However, there is a difference between how content syndication works off-line versus online. In the off-line approach, publications pay a licensing fee to the content creator, either directly or through a syndication service. In the online approach, websites pay content creators not through a financial licensing fee but through free promotion—specifically, through links back to your website.

At the bottom of every article or column you publish, you're permitted to include a brief biography for yourself and a link back to your company's website. This is the *quid pro quo* accepted by content creators and the websites that want to republish this content.

For example, when I syndicate my own articles to other sites, I end each article with a brief biography similar to this one:

> Bob Regnerus is the author of *Big Ticket eCommerce*. His marketing firm specializes in managing results-driven marketing campaigns for clients who sell high-priced products and services. He can be found online at www.bigticketcom merce.com.

Every time another website publishes my content through these online content syndication services, they include this short biography and a link along with it. This method ethically bribes other websites with the right to republish your useful content on their site, in exchange for a link back to your website. It establishes your credibility on other related websites throughout the Internet and generates traffic to your website.

If you happen to be uncomfortable with writing such content, that's no problem. Hire a writer or ghostwriter to write it for you.

3) Syndicate Content Directly to Authority Websites

The third method for getting links from authority websites also involves content syndication. However, instead of relying on content middlemen or syndication services, this strategy involves directly contacting the editors and owners of authority websites in your industry.

If your industry has a handful of websites that your prospects routinely visit, then why bother waiting for them to discover your content through a syndication service? Just contact the authority sites directly.

Imagine that a Porsche dealer contacts a website for Porsche enthusiasts, offering to provide free content, such as articles about ways to improve a car's performance or to protect its finish. In exchange, the dealer requests a two-to-four-sentence biography below the article, with a link back to the dealer's website. That link could directly lead to business, and at the very least it will improve the website's ranking.

This method requires more effort than using a third-party syndication service, but it is especially appropriate if you're in a specialized industry, where there are only a small number of well-known authority sites. If you're in more of a mass-market industry, syndication services are often a better place to start.

4) Distribute Online Press Releases

The fourth method involves publishing online press releases. You may be familiar with something similar—the traditional (off-line) press release. Off-line press releases are like prewritten articles for the media. Publications sometimes will publish these releases verbatim, but more often will use them as a basis for writing a news story. The traditional press release has historically been the communication medium of choice between the "news makers," such as big companies announcing a new product line, and the news reporters from major magazines and newspapers.

As you may have anticipated, any good off-line tool ends up finding its way online. The traditional off-line press release has also found its way online—but with a few twists.

Rather than simply serving as the news industry's communication of information to be published, press releases online often are found directly by news-seeking consumers. If you go to a major search engine or to a news search engine such as news.google.com, and search for specific news items, often you'll see the company's online press release alongside the articles written about the release.

In other words, consumers often skip a publication's interpretation of your online press release and just read it for themselves. In this way, online press releases aren't just for the press. They are also for your prospects, who often read them directly.

The second twist is that online press releases include links to your website, contained directly within the release. Whenever your online press release gets picked up and published by another website, the link to your website is automatically included. There are numerous websites that republish online press releases. Many of them only reprint press releases in a specific industry— perhaps there's one for your industry. It's worth investigating.

The industry leader in online press releases is a company called PRWeb (www.prweb.com). When you publish your release through PRWeb, it ends up on all the major news search engines, such as news.google.com and news.yahoo.com. In addition, other websites may pick up these releases and republish them on their sites— all automatically.

It's a simple way to get links back to your site and to get "votes" from authority sites, indicating that your website is one worth visiting.

The Importance of Doing Keyword Research First

When is the best time to start employing these four methods? Ideally, you should wait until after you have received some data from your pay-per-click campaign. You want the market feedback, especially information on which keywords attract qualified prospects, before making the investment of writing articles and press releases.

You want to use the keywords that your prospective buyers use. When you run a pay-per-click advertising campaign and carefully track the return on investment for *each* keyword, you find something interesting. Some keywords attract only "lookers," while other keywords attract prospects who become "buyers." Before you run a pay-per-click campaign, it's almost impossible to tell which keywords draw which type of visitors.

Without keyword research, it's also hard to tell which word choices and phrasing are most popular with prospects. For example, most insurance companies that sell auto insurance use the term "auto insurance" to describe their offerings. This is, technically, the more accurate term because "auto" refers to cars, trucks, SUVs, and minivans. Yet when you do keyword research, you discover that most consumers use the term "car insurance"—even if they happen to drive a truck or SUV, which in the insurance industry is not technically the same as a car.

So which word is the right choice to include in your content? Only by using a pay-per-click campaign can you tell for sure which phrase is more appropriate. If you guess wrong, the time and money you invest in creating content to get links may be wasted.

This is why, even for companies that get links through various forms of publishing content, I still recommend starting with pay-per-click campaigns and lead generation websites. That's the fastest way to figure out where the money is in your market.

The Trade-offs and Downsides to Internet Referrals

There are several downsides and trade-offs to generating traffic through Internet referrals. I already mentioned one of them—the lack of market insight on which keywords to build your content around.

There are a few others to keep in mind.

Some people incorrectly refer to generating Internet referrals as getting "free traffic." It's important to recognize that just because you're not paying a formal advertising bill, as you do with pay-per-click advertising, it doesn't mean you're not paying for this traffic. You still pay—but in a different way. It takes labor—your personal time or, more frequently, the time of someone you pay— to get this "free" traffic. Time is money, so there's still a cost involved.

In addition, there's a long lag time between when you begin your Internet referral efforts and when they start paying off. If you invest heavily in these efforts today, it can easily be months until you start to see results. Building your company's online reputation doesn't happen overnight.

Additionally, it's hard to make quick corrections in your course when you use referral strategies. If you spend three months creating and distributing content with the wrong keywords, you'll find out that you missed your mark—but not until three months later. In comparison, with pay-per-click advertising, when you pick the wrong keywords, you often know within a few hours or days.

To illustrate this point, let me give you an example.

In the first month of working with a new client, we'll routinely make a thousand small course corrections to a client's pay-per-click advertising campaign. In comparison, for an Internet referrals campaign, you'll be lucky to make just one course correction in the same time period.

Since the feedback loop on referral generation is so slow, the best approach is to use your targeting insight from pay-per-click to guide your efforts in Internet referral generation. This is the reason why we always start with pay-per-click campaigns and lead generation websites, even with clients for whom using Internet referrals is a natural fit.

CHAPTER 11

Traffic Strategy #4:
Repeat Visitors

Our fourth traffic strategy involves making your brochure website so useful that prospects visit it repeatedly. The repeat visitor strategy is all about getting prospects to bookmark your website and return, without any prompting from an outside advertisement or article.

Prospects who repeatedly visit your website are much more likely to buy than are those who visit just once. This shows that the prospects are seriously considering what you have to offer, but aren't quite ready to buy just yet. If you give prospects a good reason to keep coming back, they eventually warm up to the idea of buying—and often do.

This alone makes it worthwhile to focus on this strategy. It's also the reason why it's important to send first-time visitors to your lead generation website whenever possible. You get the opportunity to capture their contact information—giving you a way to communicate with them and to encourage them to return to your brochure website over and over again.

Generating repeat visitors also improves the return on your advertising investment. All of your advertising costs go into attracting a first-time visitor. If you can get the visitor to come back on his or her own, those subsequent visits are free—no paid advertising required.

It's a great free traffic strategy that enhances your other traffic investments.

Five Ways to Get Repeat Visitors

There are five effective ways to bring visitors back to your website again and again.

1) Piggyback off Your Permission-Based Email Marketing

The first way is to piggyback off your permission-based email marketing efforts. Rather than including useful information directly in your emails, you place this information on your website—using your email as a teaser to let prospects know (or to remind them) that it's there.

One of the advantages of using email marketing is timing. You're trying to catch a prospect at the moment he or she switches from being a research-oriented prospect to being an active buyer. Imagine you're a local car dealer that offers a free weekly email on fun places to visit around town (places that people have to drive to, of course). Each week the dealer emails a link back to its website, where a restaurant, park, or other place to visit is featured. For people who are always looking for interesting things to do on the weekend, this would be a genuinely useful and eagerly anticipated weekly email.

Of course, with every suggested destination, the dealer could remind prospects of new models just being released, the dealer's trade-in or trade-up program, and financing offers. Everyone who drives a car is eventually going to need a new one, and everyone who drives a car typically meets up with other people who drive cars. These are opportunities to get new customers, generate referrals, and cross-sell such services as warranty programs, parts, accessories, and services.

Perhaps the prospect wasn't interested in buying a car yesterday, but her old clunker just died today and now she's thinking she needs a new car. In the middle of this crisis, she receives the local car dealer's weekly email reminding her that it exists and can take care of her automotive needs.

Repeat traffic coupled with email marketing is a powerful way to catch prospects with the right offer at the right time.

2) Publish Relevant, Useful Information

Publishing useful FAQs and industry guides for beginners is a great way to attract repeat visitors. Your goal is to make your online guide so useful that the prospect feels compelled to bookmark it, print it out, or both.

One big tip is to make your information so overwhelmingly useful that the prospect feels as though he'd be missing out on something if he just glanced at it. Your content appears so useful and thorough that he feels compelled to come back.

Online video is a great format for this. The video must be compelling, timely, informative, and hopefully, entertaining too. For example, the car dealer mentioned in my earlier example could publish a video on how to take care of your car so it is more fuel-efficient (mentioning new fuel-efficient car models in the process) or on how to prepare for a road trip before a long weekend. Alternatively, the dealer could demonstrate government-mandated safety features required in newer cars (and why it might be a good idea to upgrade to keep your family safe). It's a great way for a prospect to build a digital relationship with you, while learning more about her options to buy.

When I'm researching a new purchasing decision, I'll occasionally stumble across a website that's incredibly useful. My first reaction is usually "Wow, I'd better bookmark this." That's the reaction you're striving for.

This method works best with permission email, as a way to remind prospects of the resources that exist on your website.

3) Publish Time-Sensitive Information

The third method for encouraging repeat customers is to include time-sensitive and relevant information on your website. Your goal is to inspire prospects to bypass search engines and your competitors' websites and instead go straight to your site for the information they need.

My previous suggestion of publishing mortgage rates on mortgage websites is a good example of this. If your industry has news or statistical information that's relevant and timely, consider publishing it.

4) Publish a Blog

A fourth way is to write an engaging blog. A blog is like a self-published newspaper column on your website. It's usually filled with a personal commentary on current topics of interest for your prospects or your industry.

If your commentary is interesting, useful, funny, or witty, prospects will come back again and again to see your most recent blog posts. Some blogs are so compelling that their readers visit the website daily or even hourly—what more could you want from a website? A blog can also foster a community of interested visitors who discuss topics with one another in the Comments section of each blog post.

If you're a small company in your field, you can create a blog in which you comment on the news made by the bigger companies in your industry. Prospects are always looking for more information to help them make sense of what's going on. Publishing a blog is one way to fulfill that need.

Blogs also happen to be a good way to get Internet referrals. If your commentary is particularly funny, insightful, provocative, or controversial, other people who publish blogs (known as "bloggers") will link to your blog and advise all their readers to read your posts. This gets targeted traffic to your website. It improves your website's rankings in the search engines.

In case you think blogging is some fringe marketing strategy, I'll tell you right now that there are even Fortune 500 CEOs who blog. The CEO of Sun Microsystems, Jonathan Schwartz, publishes a widely followed blog (http://blogs.sun.com/jonathan) on the world of technology. He even posted his company's earnings release for shareholders on his blog first, before sending it to Wall Street. In the case of the earnings announcement blog post, he wasn't selling computers or software. He was selling his company's stock—the ultimate big-ticket offer. When you look at comments from shareholders on these posts, you realize the shareholders aren't investing in Sun Microsystems stock—they're investing in Jonathan Schwartz. It's quite fascinating to see people online feel as though they've developed a personal relationship with a Fortune 500 CEO they've never actually met in person.

In the automobile industry, Vice Chairman Bob Lutz of General Motors blogs (http://fastlane.gmblogs.com/archives/bob_lutz) as an avid car buff. He loves cars and loves talking about them. When he's not helping to manage a company with 300,000 employees, he blogs. Many car enthusiasts follow his blog religiously. When something happens in the industry, they want to know what Bob Lutz thinks about it. Of course, with such a wide following, Bob Lutz naturally mentions GM trucks, cars, and company news quite often in his commentary.

If Fortune 500 CEOs and executives find it worthwhile to blog, you might want to consider it too. This is especially the case if your prospects or the people you want to influence (such as industry experts, analysts, and reporters) spend a lot of time online.

5) Create a Community Forum

The final method of generating repeat traffic involves creating a membership site or community forum where users can interact with one another. In some cases, it's worth creating separate versions of this resource—one forum for existing customers focused on customers helping one another and another forum for prospects.

This is a powerful technique, because it "outsources" content creation to a potentially massive, enthusiastic, and **free** labor force—your clients and customers. Instead of having to create all the useful information yourself, they provide it for you, helping attract other repeat visitors (not to mention free Internet referrals from the search engines). The more involved your customers are with the community, the more likely they are to consider your company first when a need arises.

You do have to be careful with this strategy. You give up a lot of control when you use prospect- and customer-generated content on your website. If your products and services stink, you will hear about it (and so will your prospects). On the other hand, if your products and services deliver amazing results, and your customers are wildly fanatical and passionate about your company, you and your prospects will hear about that too.

A community forum is one of the ultimate ways to give prospects insight into your company. If your company's goof-ups are published online for the world to see, prospects will notice this—but they'll also notice (and really believe) the good news. No company is perfect, and prospects often distrust companies that appear to be too perfect. When everything good *and* bad is published online in such forums, prospects feel as though they're seeing the whole picture—the good, the bad, and the ugly. If the good outweighs the bad and the ugly (and it better, if you want to use this strategy), then letting your customers create your content for you is quite powerful and influential.

Here's one example. There's an online forum for Honda Odyssey minivan owners and enthusiasts (www.odyclub.com). Like me, you may have had no idea such an audience existed. But the people who visit this website are exceptionally passionate about their minivans. They sign every forum post with a reference to how many Honda Odysseys they and their family members own. Go figure!

It turns out this site is a mini-authority website in the world of minivans and, in particular, the Honda Odyssey. It has nearly 30,000 articles on the site and offers 25,000 links (referral sources) from other auto-related websites. To hire writers to create 30,000 articles for you would cost millions of dollars. Hiring someone to contact and successfully convince the owners of 25,000 websites to link to your website is impossible. Last I checked, according to Google, this is the ninth most important website in the world for the keyword phrase "Honda Odyssey"—featured more prominently than the tenth most important site—www.honda.com. Interesting, isn't it?

While the most important website is Honda's dedicated Honda Odyssey website (http://automobiles. honda.com/odyssey), the enthusiasts' rank is pretty amazing nonetheless. A simple little forum is featured on Google ahead of the home page of one of the largest companies in the world!

In this case, the forum was created by customers, and it isn't affiliated with Honda or any dealer. It's too bad. Any complaints on the forum go unanswered by Honda representatives. Any news of upcoming models doesn't get promoted. If Honda created such a forum, it would enable a Honda spokesperson to become a prominent authority figure amongst the minivan enthusiasts.

If your buyers don't have such a forum, consider providing one for them. If the buyers and prospective buyers in your overall industry don't have a forum either, consider creating one for the entire industry—where you and your company get a chance to influence the conversation. If you were to create such a forum for your industry, you could become a prominent authority figure in your field.

This is a powerful strategy. Imagine all your competitors' prospects visiting your industry forum *before* they make a final buying decision. If you develop your reputation within this forum properly, you will access a large pool of prospects who might have gone unnoticed.

Considering that the software to create forums is available online for free, and that such a forum has the power to compete against the home page of a Global 500 company, developing an online forum is a strategy worth considering.

Next up, we will see one final way to generate traffic to your site: a strategy for picking a "good location."

CHAPTER 12

Traffic Strategy #5:
Picking a Good Location

The traffic strategies described so far are online variations of proven off-line marketing methods—some of which have been in use for decades or, in some cases, for centuries. Pay-per-click is a new form of classified advertising; permission-based email is 21st-century direct mail; Internet referrals are a new kind of word-of-mouth advertising; and the repeat visitor strategy is similar to the idea of creating repeat customers.

Our fifth traffic strategy is a variation of the real estate agent's maxim: "Location, location, location." I call it the "pick a good location" strategy.

Go Where the Buyers Are

In the physical world, sellers travel in packs. Malls and strip malls dot the American landscape. Where there is a McDonald's, you will usually find a Burger King nearby. Where there is a Wal-Mart, other stores will cluster. The reason is simple: If you want to sell, go where the buyers are.

For our purposes, the idea behind this strategy is to virtually "locate" a part of your business in a highly trafficked destination. It's similar to a retail chain that picks good locations for its individual stores—locations where there's a lot of foot or automobile traffic. The online version also involves picking a "good location" for your business—one where there's already a lot of Internet traffic.

There are buyers all over the Internet, of course. But there are several sites that are so popular and powerful, you are missing a prime marketing opportunity if you ignore them. The four most worth paying attention to are eBay, YouTube, Craigslist, and Amazon.

While they may not seem like a natural fit for your high-end business, there are so many buyers there with credit cards in hand that it makes sense for you to look carefully before deciding.

1) eBay

eBay (www.ebay.com) is the world's largest auction site, where sellers sell items online to the highest bidder. There are other auction sites, of course, but eBay is so dominant that all the others pale in comparison.

Certainly, eBay made its mark as the Internet's garage sale. But there's another powerful, but often ignored, way to use eBay—as a source of leads. In addition to giving away a free CD, DVD, or printed guide on your lead generation website, you can sell this guide on eBay for

$1—the lowest allowed fixed price for selling something on eBay.

For example, a travel agency selling exotic vacations wouldn't sell vacation packages on eBay. But it could sell for $1 a DVD about 12 exotic "life experience" vacations guaranteed to be the topic of conversation at your next social gathering. Each buyer of the DVD in turn becomes a prospect who might buy one more vacation package at some point down the road.

In the off-line world, banks have been doing this kind of thing for years. They set up satellite branches in grocery stores and Wal-Marts, where hundreds of prospects who need banking services gather. The satellite location provides access to prospects who might be difficult to attract to the bank's stand-alone branches.

Similarly, this strategy of promoting your almost-free information guide on eBay doesn't take the place of your primary lead generation website. Instead, it's a "satellite branch" of your lead generation website—generating leads at a place where prospects gather by the millions.

2) YouTube

YouTube (www.youtube.com) is a video sharing and social networking website. It also happens to be the fourth most popular website in the United States. It provides a free service to people and companies that want to share their online videos with the rest of the world.

Even if you haven't visited YouTube, you may know it's a site where you can view all sorts of videos that run from decidedly amateurish to broadcast network–worthy.

It is a cultural phenomenon of our time. People with video cameras and cell phones are recording their lives, and YouTube, which is now owned by Google, is storing this footage for them and sharing it with others.

But YouTube is not just a website for displaying cute videos of pet tricks. It's a place to market your products 24 hours a day, without having to pay a television network or cable channel for your measly 30 seconds. Some of the world's largest corporations are utilizing YouTube very effectively to generate buzz and increase product sales. They do so by producing entertaining, informative, and sometimes edgy videos that introduce prospects to their products. YouTube videos have been used to successfully sell things from presidential candidates (whose speeches frequently appear on the YouTube home page) to high-end kitchen blenders, and everything in between.

How does a company that's selling a worthy but seemingly unentertaining high-end product or service utilize this strategy? By telling stories. A great example is Blendtec's "Will It Blend?" campaign. It's hard to think of a product that is more commonplace than a blender, but Blendtec doesn't sell ordinary appliances. These high-end blenders will turn just about anything into a "smoothie," so the company created a series of YouTube videos, featuring a smart-alecky technician in a white lab coat who blends all kinds of random items in the company's blenders—prompting the question "Will it blend?"

These videos show Blendtec's products blending garden hoses, toilet plungers, glow sticks, garden rakes, golf clubs, and even an entire Thanksgiving dinner. The videos are ridiculously funny and attention-getting—most people can't help but share the videos with their friends. The videos also happen to demonstrate the product's unique ability to blend pretty much anything.

The company has produced more than 70 YouTube videos, which have helped to increase online sales by 500% in a single year. It's not easy to create such a compelling video or video series, but if you can pull it off, the financial payoff is substantial.

3) Craigslist

Craigslist (www.craigslist.org), an online classified ads website, is another great and probably untapped traffic source for your business. It started in 1995 as an email notification list of San Francisco events. Craigslist now publishes 30 *million* new classified ads each month that are viewed a total of *nine billion* times. It's the 12th most popular website in the United States.

It's also probably one of the simplest-looking websites on the Internet. It doesn't look like a place for a high-end business. Despite this, craigslist attracts buyers and sellers of everything, which makes it a location you cannot ignore.

For local businesses, it's an especially targeted way to attract prospects in a specific metro area. Each major city in the United States has its own version of craigslist. There's http://boston.craigslist.org for classified ads relevant to the Boston area, and http://atlanta.craigslist.org for the Atlanta metro area.

Best of all, in most cases, posting an advertisement on craigslist is *free*. The notable exceptions include charging advertisement fees for help wanted ads in 10 cities and for apartment listings in New York City.

The site is such a magnet for buyers that classified ads in local newspapers have dropped considerably in the past several years. In fact, the entire newspaper business is on the decline in large part because of the loss of classified ad revenues. When you ask industry representatives what's causing this sudden and permanent drop, they mention one name: craigslist.

If you want to go where the buyers are, it's impossible to ignore craigslist. It's free, and it's excellent for generating geographic-specific Internet traffic and prospects.

4) Amazon

Finally, let's talk about Amazon (www.amazon.com). In the first part of this book, I explained that you don't want your lead generation website to look like Amazon— a catalog website. No, I haven't changed my mind. However, you do want to work with Amazon to help you market your high-end service or product, much as you would work with eBay, YouTube, and craigslist.

Amazon is probably the most recognized eCommerce site on the Internet. It attracts more than 44 million visitors each month. You can use it to attract visitors to your lead generation website in several ways.

First, you can buy Clickriver ads, which are Amazon's own pay-per-click advertisements that appear next to search results and on product detail pages. These ads can send visitors back to your lead generation website. If there are a few prominent books about your industry that you wish you had written, do the next best thing—advertise on the Amazon listings for those books.

Another way to generate traffic from Amazon is to post book reviews about books that your ideal prospects are likely to search for. In addition, as a book reviewer, you're able to create a profile on Amazon, where you can reference your own company and website. If you take the effort to be a prominent reviewer, you can become a recognized voice among book buyers in a particular category.

Finally, you can write and publish your own book—then sell it on Amazon. Inside your book, you can reference your website, your company, and your products. While it's a lot of work, nothing beats a book for establishing yourself as a credible expert in your field. Prospects will come to respect and trust your company before they ever interact with it in person.

Amazon, craigslist, YouTube, and eBay attract such broad audiences and cost so little to use that it's foolish not to consider them. You can do worse than following the buyers and following the money.

How to Make the Most of Your Traffic

So far, I've discussed the first three steps in the Big Ticket eCommerce system: 1) creating the right strategy, 2) developing effective websites, and 3) generating traffic.

In the next chapter, I'll discuss the fourth and arguably most important step, which is to analyze and optimize the performance of the three previous steps in the Big Ticket eCommerce system.

CHAPTER 13

Step 4:
Analyze and Optimize Results

The fourth and final step of the Big Ticket eCommerce system is analysis and optimization. Analyzing and optimizing the results from the three previous steps in the system is critical to producing the overall results you want. Let me explain.

In my years of working with clients, my staff and I have generated 35 million visitors and 2.2 million leads for our clients. In each case, we followed the first three steps of what's now known as the Big Ticket eCommerce system. In every case, without exception, our first attempt at following the three steps for a client did not yield the results we were looking for. Despite being a leading expert on marketing big-ticket products and services online, my track record on the first day of a client project is almost always terrible.

Yet at the same time, somewhere between the 60th and 90th day with a new client, we double sales—in nine cases out of 10.

How can both statements be true? How can we produce uninteresting results on Day 1, yet **routinely** double sales and profits from the Internet by Day 90?

The short answer: analysis and optimization.

The long answer is that we track everything we do for our clients. We stop doing what doesn't work. We double whatever is working well. Keep that up for 90 days, along with everything else in the Big Ticket eCommerce system, and doubling sales becomes pretty typical. Analysis and optimization of your strategy, website design, and traffic generation strategies is a scientific and disciplined approach that leads to continuously improving results.

How to Double Internet Sales in 90 Days

Let me give you a simple example. Let's say on the first day of applying the first three steps of the Big Ticket eCommerce system, you produce mediocre results. Using a disciplined process of analysis and optimization, you make some small adjustments to your overall Internet effort to see if this improves results.

Let's say that by the second day. after making a few adjustments, you've improved sales by a tiny 1%. If your average sales from the Internet were $1,000 per day, they're now $1,010 per day—a less-than-dramatic growth of only $10 per day. If you're used to $100,000 a day in sales from the Internet, your sales are now $101,000 a day.

At first glance, this seems like an improvement barely worth mentioning—let alone celebrating. But if you understand the idea behind analysis and optimization, you will realize that a 1% one-day increase in sales can be a breathtaking improvement.

Here's what I mean.

Let's say on the second day of using the Big Ticket eCommerce system, you repeat the process of analyzing what worked, making some optimization adjustments, and waiting to see the next day's results. Let's assume that these changes also increased sales by only 1%. So your daily sales have grown from $1,010 to approximately $1,020 a day—or from $101,000 a day to roughly $102,000 a day—depending on which example is more appropriate for you.

Now imagine keeping this 1% daily increase in sales up for 100 days in a row. What happens? You increase sales by 100%. Yes, you *double* sales.

This isn't a rare occurrence; it's actually the norm for almost all our new clients. If you ask us to reveal the one change that caused the doubling of sales, our answer is usually that there was none. Quite often, the change was caused by a hundred tiny adjustments that added up to make a big difference.

Achieving a 1% improvement in results from the Internet on any given day is not a big deal. You could change the background color of your home page and, in some cases, see a 1% improvement in results. But imagine keeping this up for not 100 days but 1,000 days. While it does get harder and harder to find ways to improve your business by 1% a day, the concept behind the process is still quite sound.

The magic is in using a disciplined process of trying new things, tracking results, and making refinements over time.

How to Dominate a Market Using Daily Metrics

Several years ago, you could ignore your detailed daily metrics and still succeed online. Today, it's hard to win, and nearly impossible to dominate, without consistently analyzing your results and constantly optimizing your marketing efforts.

To put this in perspective, for a single client, we typically track and analyze a bare minimum of 2,000 different metrics...*daily*. More typically, we'll look at up to 10,000 such metrics...daily. In the course of 90 days, we will have analyzed and made adjustments to websites, traffic sources, and keywords based on 180,000 pieces of statistical information.

Why do we go to so much effort just to get more prospects from the Internet? We do it because it works.

If you do this, you too will see your sales increase quickly. If you're competing against a particular company whose idea of looking at metrics is asking the webmaster, "Hey! How many visitors did we get to our website last month?" you can quite easily dominate your marketplace.

Market domination isn't about magic. It's about daily discipline.

Years ago we used to do all this analysis manually. Today we use software tools to help us analyze these metrics and to assist us in making optimization decisions.

Both approaches are equally effective—though the software-assisted approach is more time-efficient.

Most companies are incredibly lazy about using analysis and optimization. When you're willing to follow a superior process and you have the discipline to stick with it, you can't help but dominate. It's not about dominating through a miracle. It's about dominating through better process executed with greater discipline.

The Incredible Power of A/B Testing

One of the "bread and butter" tools for analysis and optimization is something called A/B testing. The concept is simple.

For every aspect of your online marketing, you create two versions. One version, you call version A. The other, you call version B. You want to have two versions of your pay-per-click ads, two versions of your lead generation website, etc.

You alternate between using version A and version B of your ads, websites, and other marketing pieces. Then you compare results to determine which version performed better. Let's say the winner—version B—generated 1% more leads than the loser—version A.

The next day, you take yesterday's winner and test its effectiveness versus yet another version of your website. Perhaps you changed the headline, the offer, or the testimonials on your website. Let's say this new version beat the previous winner by an additional 1%.

You continually keep this process going every day, looking for a 1% improvement somewhere along your online marketing process. You're not looking for one big miracle improvement. A tiny 1% improvement on a regular basis will do just fine. If a 1% improvement per day is too aggressive, imagine a 1% improvement per week. That's still a 50% increase in sales every year. This is the surest path I know of to consistently increase your sales using the Internet.

Incidentally, marketers did not invent this form of disciplined experimentation—scientists did. If you happened to remember lessons from your high school science class, you might recall that each experiment you performed in science lab had a "control" group and a "test" group. This is no different than the A/B testing method I suggest you use today.

Scientists use this exact same method to invent cures for diseases and to make medical breakthroughs. If we try to stop a heart attack in progress by using version A of a new drug versus version B, which one saves more lives? If we try version B versus version C, which one saves more lives? Medical researchers do this hundreds and thousands of times in a decade to find new medical "miracles." These aren't actual miracles. These are just the result of ongoing A/B testing—a disciplined form of "trial and error"—executed consistently.

If A/B testing is the method used in medical research to figure out the most effective way to save lives, surely it's good enough to figure out the most effective way to drive more sales using the Internet.

Case Study #1:
Doubling Leads From the Internet in 60 Days

Here's an example. One of our clients had been using a lead generation website to generate and capture leads from the Internet. The site had remained the same for the past six years and had never been subjected to A/B testing. It was a fairly decent lead generation website that had no distracting links or other pages. It offered a free information guide to prospects who filled out a request form.

This particular lead generation website persuaded 13% of website visitors to fill out the lead capture form, requesting the client's free guide. As far as lead generation websites go, this isn't terrible, but the client wanted to see if we could do better.

Using design elements from the proven winners, with previous tests involving our client as our starting point, we developed a new lead generation website design. Then we implemented A/B split testing on a continuous basis to see if we could "better our best."

In this client's case, we found a number of ways to improve the site's performance. The two biggest improvements came from adding an online video to the website and from moving the free information request form to a location much closer to the top of the page. The combined impact of all these changes resulted in the site persuading 27 out of 100 visitors to fill out the lead capture form (instead of the original 13 out of 100)—doubling the site's lead generation performance without any change in advertising budget.

After our client's initial delight at doubling her company's lead flow in just six weeks, her response was "Agh…I should have done this six years ago!"

Case Study #2:
Doubling Traffic With the Same Advertising Budget

A recent client was concerned about the diminishing effectiveness of his company's Internet advertising campaigns. Despite a fairly significant and consistent monthly advertising investment, traffic to the company's website was declining steadily each month. As a short-term fix, the client was spending more and more money to maintain the same level of traffic—clearly, not a sustainable practice in the long run.

In our initial analysis, we discovered the client's pay-per-click traffic generation efforts lacked any analysis and optimization. While the client knew how much traffic his pay-per-click campaign was generating and how many leads his website was generating overall each day, he had no idea which keywords were effective and which ones were not. Having seen this situation many times, two thoughts came to mind: We knew that at least half the keywords in the campaign were money wasters, but we didn't know *which* half.

We immediately implemented a tracking, analysis, and optimization process for the client's campaigns. We were able to track how many leads each individual keyword was generating, and we discovered several keywords that were driving a lot of traffic—but not many leads. We had found the money-wasting keywords.

We immediately dropped these keywords from the client's campaign—cutting the client's advertising costs by 41%. Then we reinvested these savings in advertising under other keywords that were performing quite well. Without increasing the client's original advertising budget, we doubled the traffic to his website and doubled the number of leads generated each month.

Case Study #3:
Testing Traffic Sources to Increase Leads Tenfold

Earlier I mentioned that you should think about your eCommerce effort as building a bridge from the prospect to your company. In our first case study, the bottleneck preventing more prospects from crossing that bridge was the lack of A/B testing on the client's lead generation website. In the previous case study, the bottleneck was the lack of testing and tracking of individual keywords in a pay-per-click campaign. In this case study, you'll see that the bottleneck involved relying on a completely unproductive traffic source—Google AdWords.

One of my clients came to us after generating disappointing results from pay-per-click advertising on Google. Through our tracking and analysis, we determined that the client's Google pay-per-click campaign was attracting visitors—but those visitors were not responding to the free offer on the client's website. This offer involved a free consultation with one of the company's sales staff.

We knew the offer was a sound one because the client's off-line advertising was successful in getting prospects to take the offer. However, online visitors weren't filling out the form on the company's website. This was a problem, because the client's entire business was based on closing big-ticket purchases through telesales.

In our first attempt at tackling this problem, we were able to increase the traffic to the website, but not the number of leads generated. After a lot of experimentation, we evaluated other traffic sources and found an alternative: Advertising on specialty, industry-specific search engines was more effective than advertising on Google.

We were able to increase tenfold the number of leads generated for the client. As much as I like using Google, in this case, the numbers told us that Google simply wasn't the right fit.

Common sense would tell you that the most popular search engine should be the best advertising venue, but sometimes this isn't true. A lot of companies that try to build, maintain, and optimize their websites on their own assume that if Google doesn't work, nothing on the Internet will work. Certainly, this client had that mindset when he came to us.

Instead, we believe in tracking, analyzing, and testing different traffic sources for our clients. While we start our process with what our experience has proven to be most effective, we let the numbers from analysis and optimization guide us the rest of the way.

In this case, the numbers led us to a tenfold increase of leads from the Internet.

Case Study #4:
Generating Qualified Leads Cost-Effectively
for a $35,000 Service

In another case, my company was hired to generate leads for the executive education program at Dartmouth College's Tuck School of Business, after the school had seen the costs of advertising rise while the number of qualified leads shrank. The only advertising that was generating a significant amount of viable leads was a full-page ad in the *Wall Street Journal*, costing roughly $100,000 per day. While the advertisement was effective at generating leads, it wasn't cost-effective.

For a program that generated $25,000 to $35,000 in revenue from each student, that type of advertising was cost prohibitive. It wasn't easy to create an effective lead generation website for the program. The version of the lead generation website we ended up using differed significantly from the one we started with. We did at least 20 A/B tests on the site, all with the goal of increasing not just leads but qualified leads.

The client was running a global campaign because it wanted to attract students from overseas. However, our tracking and analysis efforts determined that leads generated from certain countries were unqualified. Since advertising to those countries consumed a significant part of the budget, we revamped the campaign to stop advertising to audiences there.

Meanwhile, we discovered that the leads coming in through traditional paid search sites—Google and Yahoo—were not of the quality that Dartmouth was seeking. We tried placing ads on about 25 secondary sites—ultimately identifying six "hidden gem" websites out of the 25. On those sites, we A/B tested 50 different advertisements to find the best-performing ad. We also pared down an initial list of about 25,000 keywords to just 2,000 highly profitable and productive keywords. It took about six months, but the results were extraordinary.

This effort has dramatically increased the leads generated by Dartmouth's advertising. Cost per lead has been significantly more cost-effective than the *Wall Street Journal* ads. Feedback from the executive education program's sales staff shows that the prospects generated are exactly the kind of serious prospect they were hoping for. We'll hear back from them in a few months on actual sales results, since Dartmouth's admission schedule accepts applications only at specific times during the year, but so far all client objectives have been met.

The "Fail Fast and Cheap" Approach to Increasing Sales

What you'll notice about this last case study is the sheer volume of testing involved—25 traffic sources tested (only six cost-effective sources discovered), 50 different advertisements tested (only one "most effective" advertisement discovered), and 25,000 keywords tested (only 2,000 "most productive" keywords discovered). In a purely statistical sense, nine out of 10 things didn't work (or didn't work as well as the "something" we discovered later).

Thankfully, the process of analysis and optimization allows you to get rid of the things that don't work. It's like taking a 10-question test in school, realizing you got only one answer right, and then legitimately erasing the nine questions you got wrong. You end up with a perfect score every time. This is exactly how the analysis and optimization process works.

The key to getting the Big Ticket eCommerce system to work for you isn't necessarily getting things right on the first day. It's about consistently trying many different things, and consistently getting rid of what's not working—leaving you with a "perfect score" every time.

In fact, the real secret to successful tracking, analysis, and optimization is to "fail" quickly and cheaply. Remember those 50 advertisements we tested for Dartmouth? We ran some of them for only a day—in some cases, investing only $50 or $100 to find out which ads didn't work as well as some other ad we tried. Remember those 25,000 keywords we tested? Some keywords cost a whopping $2 to test before we discovered that we should ban them from our list permanently. In the end, we had a lead generation process that was surprisingly productive and cost-effective.

If you're not testing many different approaches in your Internet efforts, I can tell you right now that you're wasting money—or at the very least, letting slip through your fingers the extra leads that you could have gotten at no additional cost.

Consistent, disciplined tracking, analysis, and optimization always leads to better results...*always*. It's not a concept, a theory, or an idea. It's just pure math.

It's never wrong. It just takes some time and discipline to become right.

Disciplined Habits Versus Technique of the Month

One of the trends I see among many companies looking to do business online is an infatuation with and intimidation by what I call the "technique of the month." Because the Internet changes so rapidly, there's always some new marketing or traffic technique being invented that you're not using yet. Some companies feel enormous pressure to appear as though they are on the cutting edge—using the latest technique. Other companies simply become intimidated and overwhelmed by yet another buzzworthy technique they aren't using.

Personally, I think neither reaction is the right one. You shouldn't be using some new marketing fad just because it's the "cool" thing to do. You shouldn't be ignoring it entirely either. In fact, I think the whole focus on cutting-edge techniques is highly overrated.

This is the equivalent of the dieting industry's latest fad diet. There's the grapefruit diet, the no-fat diet, the no-carb diet, the chocolate diet, and numerous others. To date, nobody has really come up with anything better than the stop-eating-junk-and-eat-healthy-and-exercise-daily **habit.**

The same is true of eCommerce and online marketing. There will always be some fad or hot buzzword that you're not using. This is, frankly, okay by me. Good habits, or in our case a good **process,** wins in the end. You don't ignore these new techniques. You simply apply them within the context of a disciplined process. In our case, the most important ongoing process you must use is the tracking, analysis, and optimization of your Internet efforts.

Optimizing End-to-End Internet Efforts: A Strategic Approach

Here's another trend I see that's terribly unproductive. A lot of employees you may hire, or firms you may outsource to, take an overly narrow view of Internet commerce and marketing. You have the email marketing specialist, the SEO specialist, the social media specialist, and the "technique-of-the-month" specialist.

The problem with the people and firms that take such a narrow view of their role is they completely miss the "big picture." The only thing that matters is increasing sales. Sales don't increase because of some new technique. Sales increase by getting the whole system to function well holistically.

As we've discussed, a good Internet strategy is like building a bridge. The purpose of a bridge is to get someone from one side to the other—in this case, to get the prospect from the marketplace to your company, where he or she will buy a high-priced product or service. Imagine that an effective bridge requires 10 segments to accomplish this objective. Assume that some employee or firm you've hired has some new way to "improve" the eighth segment of your bridge—a segment that happens to be working fine already. What's the point of this new technique if your bridge has collapsed in segments two and three and nobody on your team has the breadth of perspective to realize this?

It isn't easy to find a person or a firm with the skills and breadth of experience required to see this "big picture." Yet without this strategic perspective and approach, it's hard to get the best results possible.

Don't ask a sales-oriented person for guidance; he just thinks about the end of this process—closing the sale without much input on how to start the process. If you ask a webmaster, she's only concerned with how the website looks. A copywriter is concerned with the words on the page, but is not interested in how the traffic sources influence results. A programmer worries about the code used to run the website, but as long as the website doesn't crash, everything is good. The graphic designer wants the site to look nice—and ignores any statistical data that proves his design reduces sales.

A search engine optimization company wants lots of free traffic—but if you can't turn that traffic into leads and then sales, that's not the company's problem. After all, it got you more traffic for "free." The pay-per-click consultant just wants to drive traffic. But what happens if your sales force can't close those leads? Perhaps pay-per-click isn't the way to go at all—of course, this never occurs to a pay-per-click specialist.

When you deal with so many narrowly focused specialists, it's like handing a kid a hammer—suddenly, everything starts to look like a nail. It never occurs to the kid that maybe a saw or a drill might be a more useful tool given the big picture—the overall goal. Instead, a kid with a hammer just wants to hammer things. Internet "specialists" are often the same way.

It's important for you to personally guard against this type of narrow thinking. The only thing that matters is increasing sales and profits. This requires your entire strategy to work—to get prospects all the way across that bridge you're building. Every narrowly focused "technique" specialist can give you only a partially correct (and partially incorrect) answer to any question you pose. You can't let these narrow specialists convince you to use their favorite type of "hammer" whenever there's a problem. You have to optimize your end-to-end efforts strategically. That strategy is the only thing driving the results you want—so it's the only thing that matters.

Section II:
Getting Started

CHAPTER 14

Deciding Where and How to Start

For companies with brand-new eCommerce projects, the natural starting point for the Big Ticket eCommerce system is at Step 1—creating a strategy. For most companies that already have some or even a significant Internet presence, it's more difficult to decide where to start.

In this situation, let me make two suggestions: (1) Start by analyzing the big picture to find the problems in your previous online efforts, and (2) focus your efforts on the area that offers the biggest potential for improvement while requiring the least effort.

Start With a Physical Before Calling the Heart Surgeon

Most HMO medical insurance companies require you to get an annual physical before ever letting you call in the heart surgeon. There's actually a sound reason for doing this: When you skip ahead to focus on a specific problem before taking a look at the big picture, you run the risk of spending a lot of money to solve the wrong problem.

I'll argue that the same is true when it comes to the Internet. Before immediately grabbing on to the idea of investing in some new buzzworthy technique or hot trend, it's a good idea to evaluate the basics.

When you have a clear sense of the big picture, you get a clear sense of how your eCommerce system is doing. You want to check all the major vital signs of your Internet efforts. Measure your numbers in certain areas, and compare them against what's considered "normal" and healthy. If your numbers come back too high or too low, this may provide a clear indication of which problem is most instrumental in holding back your sales and profits.

More than anything, resist the temptation to jump ahead, and avoid solving a "problem" you don't really have. I see this all the time with prospective clients. They're so eager to hire us to drive more traffic to their websites that I often have to rein them in a little and ask, "What makes you think you have a traffic problem?"

You'd be surprised. Probably half of the time, the problem that prospective clients think they have is actually just a symptom of the real underlying problem.

When you visit your medical doctor to complain about a symptom, it's irresponsible for the doctor to treat your symptoms without first figuring out what's causing them. The headache you're complaining about could be from stress, dehydration, or a brain tumor. It's useful—actually, critical—to know which problem you're facing. You don't want brain surgery to solve your symptom if two aspirin will do. Similarly, in trying to improve your Internet marketing efforts, it's important to know what underlying problem is causing the visible symptoms you don't like.

Again, you don't want to waste time and money trying to solve a problem you don't have. I can't emphasize this point enough. It happens so often, and it's just a complete waste of money—not to mention terribly frustrating for business owners and executives.

Common Problems and Their Related Symptoms

In a moment, I'll share with you issues we commonly see in each of the four steps of the Big Ticket eCommerce system. I'll also explain why these symptoms often mask an entirely different, underlying problem. You'll see why many people get confused by the situation and end up focusing their efforts in the wrong area.

Before we get into these specific problems, let me explain where my perspective comes from. Most of our client work involves steps 3 and 4 of the Big Ticket eCommerce system—generating traffic and then analyzing and optimizing the results from that traffic. Despite this, we start all new client work with an audit— an overall evaluation of the client's business. We do this for several reasons:

1. To make sure we understand how our contribution fits into the client's overall business (even if we're working on just one part of the

"bridge," we want to make sure our part connects
well to the other parts)

2. To ensure that we're solving the right problem
    for the client

3. To determine whether what the client has asked
    us to do will actually improve sales or other
    performance metrics

Interestingly, we did not always insist on starting with
an audit. In the past, what often happened was that we
did exactly what the client wanted us to do—but the
client wasn't happy. The client didn't get the desired
outcome, even though we delivered on everything we
were asked to do. The problem, we later discovered, was
that the client asked us to do the wrong thing!

I suppose there's a reason why heart surgeons don't let
patients decide where to cut with a scalpel. Well, we
learned that the hard way, and now we insist on doing an
audit first. We've found it to be in the client's best
interest, and it also protects our reputation and track
record.

By performing these audits, we have uncovered many
of the hidden problems that I'll be sharing with you
shortly. If a client's request is doomed to fail, these audits
allow us to stop it from ever getting off the ground.
Instead, we work with our clients to evaluate the true
issue and to make adjustments that significantly improve
the chances of success.

When we started this audit process, it consisted of
looking at 10 specific areas of a client's business. Over
time, as occasional hidden problems sneaked through our

audit, we analyzed what our audit missed and improved on it (our own internal form of the analysis and optimization step). We've continually refined our audit process, and we now evaluate 52 specific items in a client's eCommerce effort. We have also developed our own proprietary scoring system that rates a company's Big Ticket eCommerce effectiveness in a scale from 0 to 100. When a company scores a 0, it's doing nothing right at all. If the company scores 100, it's doing everything right.

In performing these audits, we've noticed several dozen problems. While space limits us from going into all of them, let's look at a few of the more common ones. You'll get a feel for what we notice in certain eCommerce efforts that others often miss. This will help you avoid similar problems in your own business.

Common Problem #1:
Skipping Steps in the Big Ticket eCommerce System

One common mistake that's made by many companies is skipping steps in the Big Ticket eCommerce system— particularly the first step, developing a strategy. For example, the two most common requests we hear from clients are:

1. I want a lead generation website.

2. I need more traffic and leads.

In these cases, many of the clients we see haven't clearly thought through their overall strategy. For example, companies will say they want a better website or more traffic. Yet when we ask them certain questions, we get answers that show a lack of integration or consideration of the "big picture" issues needed to actually increase sales.

For example, we'll ask, how do you close the leads that you generate online? Why did you decide on that particular method? What method generates the most off-line sales for you? Why are the two methods different?

Here's what happens when a company struggles under this rigorous examination of its eCommerce effort. When we ask the client why a particular choice was made, often the reply is "Isn't that what everyone else is doing?"

The problem with this thinking is that it doesn't take into consideration the company's unique assets. It's a "me too" approach that blindly copies everyone else, rather than strategically asking, "What's a unique asset in the company that we can take advantage of in this situation?"

Do you want to build a big email list or generate a lot of inbound telephone calls to your call center? Why have you chosen one or the other as your goal?

Do you want to generate leads online and market to the prospects off-line? Or do you want to do the reverse: generate leads off-line and market to them online? Why? What's the rationale? What are you trying to accomplish by doing that?

A strategy is about fitting together all the pieces of a puzzle so you get the results that you want. If the pieces don't fit together, even if one piece is particularly good, sales and profits do not grow. Your online efforts have to link together with your off-line efforts. The psychological profiling of the ideal prospect has to drive the keyword research. The keyword research has to drive the pay-per-click campaign design. The pay-per-click campaign has to drive A/B testing, analysis, and optimization of the lead generation website. The lead capture form on your website must feed your company's most productive sales process. All the pieces of the puzzle must fit together.

The strength of a strategy is much like that of a chain: as weak as its weakest link. When you try to build a bridge from the marketplace to your company, if part of the bridge is missing, prospects can't get across. A strategy can't be missing any critical pieces. All the elements that go into a strategy must be decided with the big picture in mind. It's all got to work together, and when you skip steps—especially the strategy step—it can't.

Common Problem #2:
Making Decisions Based on Opinions Versus Numbers

A client says to me, "I'd like you to add the company's corporate logo to the lead generation website."

Instead of the "Yes, no problem" answer the client is expecting, we respond by asking, "Why do you want to add a logo?"

The client replies, "The site looks so plain without it."

My response: "Is your goal to have a website with your company logo on it or to generate more leads?"

The reply: "Can't we do both?"

My reply: "We A/B tested two versions of your lead generation website—one with the company logo and one without it. The version without the logo generated more leads."

Client: "Can't we put the logo on there anyway?"

Me: "Sure, we can, but are you sure you want to deliberately decrease sales?"

Client: "No…but let's put the logo on there anyway."

I've had countless variations of this conversation with clients over the years. It seems so illogical, yet it's quite common.

You can make decisions in one of two ways: (1) based on your opinions and guesses, or (2) based on the numbers. Needless to say, if you're serious about increasing the sales of your high-priced products and services, I recommend making decisions based on the numbers.

While just about everyone agrees with this in concept, in reality many people have a hard time with it. Often what the numbers tell us to do is counterintuitive—it goes against our opinion or what we thought was true.

This poses the following dilemma for many people: Is it better to acknowledge that your opinion was wrong and increase sales, or to stick with your opinion and decrease sales? Surprisingly, for a lot of people it's more important to stick with their opinion.

As for me, one of the reasons my firm is so effective at increasing sales is that we're willing to let the numbers prove us wrong—so long as we increases sales as part of the process.

For example, one of the services we provide to clients is to develop a lead generation website on their behalf. Our lead generation website development methodology is based on the extensive testing of nearly 100,000 lead generation website formats and elements. We're able to test so many website design elements with the help of automated tracking and testing tools.

We don't think we know what works; we factually know what works when it comes to lead generation websites.

Here's a small sample of the many website design elements we've tried over the years:

- Showing one headline versus another

- Putting the website form on the left versus the right side of the page

- Using an online video on the home page versus not using a video

- Using a video that plays by itself versus a video where you must hit the play button

- Placing a website form button that's capitalized as "SUBMIT" versus "Submit"

- Comparing a headline in red text versus black text

- Trying a web page with a wide format versus one with a narrow format

- Testing a website with an all-black background versus an all-white background

- Putting the lead capture form at the very top of the home page versus at the bottom

- Trying one particular phrasing of a free offer versus an alternative phrasing

- Offering a "Free Report" versus a "Free Guide"

- Testing a "Free Report" versus a "Free Report ($29 Value)"

- Putting a company logo at the top versus no company logo

- Comparing a five-page website to a one-page website

This illustrates the kind of data-driven decision process you should consider adopting in your online efforts. I suspect this approach is difficult for some people to accept, because they're not used to having so much factual information at their disposal. This is one of the amazing breakthroughs realized by the Internet. With the entire Internet being digital, you can track, analyze, and optimize literally everything.

Try doing the same thing in a retail store with 20 different employees—it's much, much more difficult. Off-line, data is hard to collect; A/B testing is even harder. Online, it's all easy to do. And when you do gather data and use it, you can consistently make profitable decisions.

Let the numbers be your guide. This is the surest path to increasing your sales.

Common Problem #3:
Forcing a Brochure Website to Be Your
Primary Lead Generation Website

A common mistake we frequently see is a company trying to force a brochure website to serve as the primary lead generation website. Remember, every tool solves a particular problem. Hammers solve one kind of problem—saws, another. Brochure websites solve a particular problem that's quite different from the one solved by a highly focused lead generation website.

In most cases, you need both website types in order to be successful. In some cases, just having a lead generation website is sufficient (especially if you have a very well-established off-line sales and marketing operation). Under no circumstances is having just a corporate brochure site adequate for maximizing sales of big-ticket offerings.

When you rely on only a brochure website for lead generation, you typically see that the number of website visitors who become prospects is low—perhaps one or two visitors out of 100 become leads. When you have this type of website and poor results like these, it's almost always because you're using the wrong type of website. The dedicated lead generation website is the better way to go.

Here's just one simple reason why dedicated lead generation websites outperform brochure websites by 20 to 50 times: links. The typical brochure website has a dozen or so links on the home page. That gives the visitor 12 different things to do, other than filling out your lead capture form.

If you've ever been to Disneyland or Disney World, there are two things you notice when you finish an amusement ride. The first is, there's only one exit. The second is, the exit always leads you to the gift shop. Trust me, this is not an accident. I have the credit card receipts to prove it.

There's a reason there aren't 12 exits to each ride, only one of which exits toward the gift shop. When you give people 12 choices, not surprisingly, their choices will be distributed among the 12 options. Give them just one choice, on the other hand, and you get more visitors to do what you want them to do. For Disney, that involves selling souvenirs. For you, that means getting people to fill out your lead capture form on your dedicated lead generation website.

The more choices there are, the fewer the number of people that end up picking any one choice. It's common sense. If there's only one "choice," they tend to take it. It works for Disney. It can work for you.

Common Problem #4:
Focusing on Traffic Without Analysis and Optimization

People with a website know they need traffic. But most people don't think they need to perform analysis and optimization. This disconnect is a big mistake. Attempting to generate traffic without tracking your results, analyzing your data, and making adjustments is like driving a car blindfolded. Sure, you're making "progress," but you have no idea where you're going, whether you're on track, or when you've reached your destination.

You would never drive your car blindly, so why would you generate traffic to your website blindly?

It's equally important to analyze and optimize your performance metrics based on the outcome you want to achieve. It always drives me nuts when someone says, "We had a great month online. We got 100,000 hits to the website." My response is "Who cares? What were the revenues and profits?"

Pay-per-click specialists tend to optimize to get you the most clicks for the lowest amount of money. Email marketing specialists optimize for esoteric things such as "open rates." Search engine optimization specialists focus on website rankings. Programmers optimize their code to ensure that your website doesn't crash. Copywriters optimize the words on the page so they're persuasive to visitors. But where in all this is someone optimizing to get the maximum revenue and profits from your Internet efforts? That's the most important thing! Yet ironically, it's the metric that the fewest people pay attention to.

Don't let the people who optimize anything other than sales and profits cloud your judgment. While these kinds of specialists play a useful role, they should not be making your business decisions for you. Sound business judgment and common sense work as well online as they do offline. Don't let any technical specialist or buzzword specialist convince you otherwise.

Also, insist that the people on your team focus on the numbers you (not they) want to optimize for—typically, sales and profits. Whatever you do, never optimize for some buzzword you can't pronounce or understand. The Internet isn't rocket science. It's just business with a few technical elements to it.

Common Problem #5:
Thinking eCommerce Is a Project,
When It's Actually a Process

Most companies have an eCommerce or website project. Few have a very good eCommerce process. The former suggests that you do something and then you're done. The latter suggests it's an ongoing effort.

In this book, I've outlined the key elements of a proven process for increasing your sales of high-priced products and services. I hope you will resist the natural tendency to turn your Internet efforts into a project. So try not to say to yourself, "We need a new lead generation website creation project." Instead, try to say, "We need to put in place a proven, ongoing process to generate leads from the Internet."

When it comes to your team, insist that they think and act this way too. If they're overly project oriented, you need to show them that it's really a process. Insist that your vendors operate in the same way.

In many ways, growing your sales from the Internet is like raising children. You don't have a one-time "raise a child" project. Instead, you do something called "parenting"—it's an ongoing process. The same is true for increasing sales using the Internet—it too is a process.

Start by Fixing the Biggest Problem First

Once you have a clear evaluation of your overall eCommerce system, it's time to decide where to focus first. When we perform audits for our clients, the rule of thumb we recommend is to fix the biggest problem first. Or, in today's politically correct terminology, focus on the area with the biggest "opportunity for improvement."

For example, if during an audit we find that a client has a decent website and reasonable online advertisements but terrible keyword research, we suggest starting there. It's not worth improving a website or getting more traffic when the keyword research is wrong. You're just going to invest more money without actually improving sales. If the client initially came to us looking for an ongoing traffic generation effort, we would probably tell the client to start with the keyword research first.

Let's look at another example. If during an audit we find that a client has no analysis and optimization process in place, we'll counsel the client to start with that problem first. Forget about trying to increase your traffic initially; just get your tracking, analysis, and optimization process in place. Stop wasting so much money. Fix that gaping hole in your eCommerce efforts, and then come back a few weeks later to increase overall traffic.

If during an audit we discover that a client has a mismatch between how he captures leads and how his sales force is accustomed to selling to leads, we'll suggest that the client fix the mismatch first—before trying to increase website traffic. For example, assume that the client's website captures leads using a website form—yet the company's entire sales department is accustomed to closing sales by telephone. This is an obvious mismatch between how the online portion of the business connects to the company's off-line assets—in this case, its stellar telephone sales force. There's no point in starting by trying to drive more traffic to a website if the lead handoff mechanism isn't working. Fix the handoff first. Then drive more traffic. You'll see a greater increase in sales more quickly and with less effort.

In addition to deciding where to get started with Big Ticket eCommerce, an equally important decision involves whom to get started with. We cover the important topic of picking the right team in the next chapter.

CHAPTER 15

How to Build Your Big Ticket eCommerce Team

Imagine you have set a goal of climbing to the top of Mount Everest, the tallest mountain peak in the world. Many people attempt this goal, but few succeed. Some even die trying. Climbing Everest is serious business. How would you approach this challenge, when your life would literally depend on the outcome?

Most people start by wondering about the best way to get to the top. Surely with all the trial and error—or in some cases, trying and dying—there must be a best way. There must be common life-threatening mistakes to avoid. There must be a best time of year to try. There must be a proven path.

If the person who had been to the top of Everest the most times had written a book on the topic, you'd get that book and study it a dozen times. Doing anything short of that would be suicidal. However, if all you did was read that book, it wouldn't be enough. The right system, method, or approach is useless without a good team that will put to use what you know. Pick your mountain-climbing team well, and your chances of success and survival improve dramatically. Pick poorly, and you're likely to end up frustrated by failure, or worse...dead.

The same is true when it comes to driving sales of your big-ticket offerings. This book provides you with a proven approach to reach your highest goals. It is based on real-world experience, often painfully discovered. It's the accumulation of 100,000 educated trial-and-error attempts, and it gives you the best approach without incurring the cost of trying the 99,999 less-effective approaches.

However, despite all this, without a strong team, you won't achieve your goal. To get the job done, it takes a mix of a strong in-house team and, in most cases, a strong outsourced team too.

The 12 Roles Needed to Grow Big-Ticket Sales

In this chapter, I'll outline the 12 key roles that are required to drive sales using the Internet. Let me start by making two important points related to staffing your team.

First, you'll notice that, while you need to fill all the following roles to be successful, not all are full-time roles, especially in medium-sized or even smaller businesses. In these cases, it's impossible to justify paying a full-time salary when your needs for that particular role are only part time. In these cases, outsourcing can often be an attractive and cost-effective advantage. You get someone whose skills stay sharp from full-time engagement in a particular role, but you don't have to cover the full cost yourself. I mention this for the benefit of those who, when they read here that they need 12 roles filled, worry because they can't possibly justify a 12-person headcount in their Internet marketing organizations.

Second, I would encourage you to think about your team in terms of roles first, people second. For example, two important roles are the keyword researcher and the pay-per-click campaign manager. You want to think about your team according to each person's formal role. The alternative, of course, is to think of your team based on the names of the people you have on staff: I have John and Mary. Which roles can I force them to take? Instead, decide on the roles you want, then decide on the in-house person or outside resource that is the most appropriate for that role. Don't let your existing staff drive your staffing strategy. Let your staffing strategy drive your staffing decisions. It's a useful point to keep in mind.

Let's start by discussing the most important leadership role, the eCommerce Executive.

Role #1:
The eCommerce Executive

In large companies, the eCommerce executive is the person who holds the vice president of eCommerce or some other similar title. It's the executive in charge of driving financial results by harnessing the Internet. In medium-sized companies, this is often the CEO or business owner.

The person in this role has sound business judgment and thinks of eCommerce as just another way to drive sales or profits. This person thinks in terms of results and the bottom line. Clicks, hits, and impressions are nice, but profitable sales matter more.

This person needs a strong conceptual understanding of Big Ticket eCommerce, but does not need to get bogged down in the details. The executive recognizes that there are four steps to this process and can ensure that all four steps are followed in the order outlined, even if he or she doesn't have the technical skills to perform any one step in the process.

The executive needs to be a strategic thinker who considers the big picture. This should be a person who is concerned less about the technical details of each particular piece of the bridge and more about overall results.

Finally, the person in this role is the chief recruiting officer for your eCommerce efforts. The executive seeks out the people and firms to fill the required roles. This is also the person who will make that tough call when a certain person or firm isn't the right choice, given your company's needs. The eCommerce executive recognizes that roles come first, and individual people and firms come second.

Role #2:
Internet Marketing Strategist

Your team also needs an Internet marketing strategist. This is someone who thinks of the big picture, as the eCommerce executive does, but also has a strong technical grasp of all the pieces within the Big Ticket eCommerce system. The eCommerce executive figures out where the company wants to go with its online efforts; the Internet marketing strategist figures out how to get there.

There is no substitute for experience in this role. You want someone who has made mistakes and learned from them. You want someone who knows the rules and the exceptions to the rules.

This person must know how to define, manage, and track a campaign and to make sure the numbers add up. In addition, the strategist must understand the roles of everyone else on the team: how to do keyword research to attract prospects; how to design the lead generation websites; how to analyze the pay-per-click campaigns; how to evaluate advertisement costs, click-through rates, conversions, and costs per lead; and so on. The strategist also must be skilled in making decisions based on the data.

This role is an extensive one whenever you're starting an eCommerce effort from scratch, or contemplating a major shift or improvement. This is the person who helps you figure out that you may be heading in the wrong direction—and shows you how to head in the right one.

On an ongoing basis, this role is limited only to "check-ins" and evaluations of progress. The strategist ensures that changes in the marketplace don't disrupt progress and verifies that all major actions continue to be the right ones.

Role #3:
Project Manager

The project manager coordinates the day-to-day activities of most of the other roles. This person has a solid understanding of Big Ticket eCommerce concepts and a mid-level understanding of the technical details.

For example, our project managers, who manage our clients' work, can all recognize what terrible keyword research looks like but don't have the skills to create good keyword research. They know enough to recognize a flawed website design but don't have the technical skills to create a good one. Of course, they can recognize a good design—if it has been created by someone else.

This person doesn't make the big decisions but ensures that the big decisions are followed and executed on time. The project manager manages resources, schedules activities, and flags problems to be addressed by the eCommerce executive and the Internet marketing strategist.

Role #4:
Keyword Researcher

Keyword researchers must be able to understand intimately your company's products or services, as well as the motivations, hopes, and dreams of your customers. Using the best tools available and his or her own personal intuition, a researcher must determine the most effective keywords to help search engines find your website. As with other personnel, experience is the key.

Good keyword researchers are an unusual breed. They are a blend between an FBI profiler and someone with a PhD in linguistics. They are able to get inside the heads of your prospects to uncover how they think and act. They're also able to connect those psychological insights and match them to specific phrasing of words, recognizing the subtle but important distinction between people who search for similar, but not identical, phrases.

Keyword researchers make lousy dates and dinner companions. If you take them out to dinner, they're studying what you say and what you do, and they're secretly writing keyword ideas on napkins to add to their keyword lists.

If you have a real keyword researcher on staff, you'd definitely know it. If you have to wonder if someone on your staff can fill the keyword researcher role, the fact that you even have to wonder shows that the person doesn't have the DNA for this kind of work. It's a highly specialized skill. It's similar to the distinction between, say, a medical doctor who is a general practitioner and one who is a surgeon. Only in the case of keyword researchers, they're so specialized that they're the equivalent of a cardiac surgeon who operates only on infants—not just any surgeon, but a pediatric cardiac surgeon.

As with most highly specialized fields, experience matters a lot. For example, the junior keyword researchers on my staff research and come up with 300,000 keywords a year. My most senior keyword researcher has been doing this work for eight years, and has researched nearly 3 million keywords in his career. If the person you have in mind has not generated at least 750,000 keywords in his or her career, keep looking. Your entire traffic generation effort is built on the foundation of this keyword research. When you're trying to build a 100-story skyscraper, you don't put a rookie structural engineer in charge of designing the building's foundation. You want a veteran.

Role #5:
Pay-Per-Click Campaign Manager

A pay-per-click campaign manager must be able to manage sophisticated and complex online advertising campaigns. For example, our pay-per-click campaign managers manage several hundred advertisements; review 5,000 to 10,000 keywords grouped into hundreds of categories and dozens of campaigns; and generate and analyze more than 5,000 pieces of performance data per day—for just one client.

Pay-per-click traffic in particular generates an enormous amount of highly useful statistical data. This data must be processed and analyzed consistently in order to identify opportunities to exploit and money-losing efforts to shut down.

A pay-per-click campaign manager has the mentality and mind-set of an air traffic controller or a commodities exchange floor trader; this person evaluates small changes in market data by the minute and can make decisions quickly.

For the pay-per-click campaign manager, the ability to make the right decision resides in the numbers. The only problem is that there are a lot of numbers to consider, and they change daily.

In addition to being able to make numbers-based marketing decisions, the campaign manager must write short pay-per-click advertisements. Writing a full-page ad or using 1,000 words to convey an idea is easy. It's much harder to convey the same idea in 10 words. Suddenly, tiny changes take on major significance. For example, do you capitalize the first letter of your website address or use all lowercase? When you have to get the job done with only a few letters and words, every tiny detail makes a statistical difference. Your campaign manager must have the skills to consider this and act accordingly.

Experience also matters for this role. Our pay-per-click campaign managers are all required to have managed $500,000 in advertising investments per year before I hire them, retrain them, and mentor them—and then they're allowed to work on our clients' campaigns.

One million dollars per year in advertising may not seem like a lot, but when you're using an advertising medium that allows you to track where every dime goes, that's a lot of dimes to keep track of—10 million dimes per year to be exact, or roughly 27,000 dimes to count and track daily.

Role #6:
Internet Referral Maker

The Internet referral maker's role is to get other websites and search engines to refer more traffic and qualified visitors to your website. This role involves two key areas.

First, it involves improving your brochure website to make it "referral friendly." This consists of some technical things that make it easy for other websites and search engines to refer visitors to you. The other key aspect of the role is developing a large Rolodex of influential websites.

An Internet referral maker knows how to find the websites that are influential and powerful referral sources, distinguishing them from sites that are a waste of time. Like any word-of-mouth marketing effort, getting more referrals online is about having something interesting to say, and then getting the most important websites to recognize it and pass it along to others. During this process, visitors are referred to your website. The role of the Internet referral maker encompasses generating referrals from search engines, press release services, online article syndication services, and the powerful authority sites in your industry.

To fill the Internet referral maker roles on our staff, we start by looking for people who have the natural inclination to reach out to other people. Instead of just relying on their personal Rolodex of influential websites, our Internet referral makers use a firm-wide shared Rolodex. This means that the one amazing referral source we found for a client a year ago can be reused today by an unrelated client.

Our Rolodex of referral sources is one of the most carefully guarded assets we use when working on Internet referrals on behalf of our clients. Whether you leverage someone else's Rolodex or build your own, it's an important asset for generating Internet referrals.

Role #7:
"Virtual Real Estate" Agent

When it comes to picking a good location in the off-line world, you use a real estate agent. When it comes to picking a good "virtual real estate" location for a branch of your online business, the same is true.

The virtual real estate agent must understand the various traffic patterns of the highest-traffic websites in the world. As discussed earlier, virtual real estate properties you'll want to consider for your company include eBay, YouTube, craigslist, and Amazon. In many cases, you can establish a small presence—a virtual satellite office—for free or for next to nothing.

Each of the major online real estate "locations" appeals to a different type of prospect. A good virtual real estate agent can help match your ideal prospect to the right location. The agent can also set up your satellite office presence within these high-profile locations. In addition, the agent should keep a lookout for emerging locations that show high-potential commercial value.

The virtual real estate agents on our staff work with clients to buy, often at little to no cost, virtual real estate on these properties.

Role #8:
Analysis and Optimization Engineer

While every phase of the Big Ticket eCommerce system can be subjected to tracking, analysis, and optimization, it's essential to have at least one person focusing on optimizing the end-to-end process. Remember, it's not about getting a click. It's about getting a sale.

One of the primary roles of the analysis and optimization engineer is to A/B test the design elements of our clients' lead generation websites. Despite the extensive testing we've done to come up with our lead generation website designs, we still continue to test relentlessly.

For one thing, the Internet is continually changing. While we have found a dozen or more specific website elements to be unusually productive in generating leads, how you combine these elements for a particular market does change the results you get. The analysis and optimization engineer tests new website design elements and new combinations of preexisting elements on each client's lead generation website.

The analysis and optimization engineer orchestrates all the A/B tests throughout the system and ensures that the discoveries are passed along to key team members, with the ultimate goal of delivering the specific outcome our clients expect.

The engineer needs to have a strong understanding of the marketing principles behind the Big Ticket eCommerce system. This person must be able to leverage an extensive history of test data and calculate what combinations of website elements generate the most leads. The individual needs a strong background in mathematics and statistical analysis, as well as the ability to focus on the big picture.

Role #9:
Lead Generation Copywriter

The copywriter creates the words on the lead generation website that convince prospects to say "yes" to your offer of a free guide, report, or other educational materials. The copywriter, more than anything, is a salesperson who sells through the written word. The person in this role takes guidance from the rest of the team about what to focus on and emphasize.

The Rest of the Team

The remaining three roles needed for your team are more typical to the Internet marketing industry. With the exception of the eCommerce executive, all the previously identified roles can be outsourced to client service firms such as mine. However, the next three roles should be managed in-house on either a full-time or a part-time basis, depending on your needs and the work volume. These roles are as follows:

Role #10: The *webmaster* administers technical website changes and updates website content.

Role #11: The *permission-based email marketing manager* writes and sends email marketing messages to prospects. This person's role is to send content that keeps prospects engaged and encourages them to take the next step in your sales process—book a meeting, make a phone call, or whatever appropriate step you designate.

Role #12: The *content writer* produces content for your website articles and press releases. This content can be reused by the email marketing manager and the webmaster, and can be handed off to the Internet referral maker for wider distribution throughout the Internet. The content writer needs to be able to explain and teach through words, but need not be a master salesperson.

Beware the "Square Peg, Round Hole" Problem

Another situation to avoid is something I call the "square peg, round hole" problem. It's the idea that you force existing staff members to fit into roles they aren't qualified to fill. It's like taking someone with steady hands, handing him a scalpel and a heart surgery manual, and telling him to cut open your chest and perform open-heart surgery. You certainly wouldn't make that staffing decision if your life depended on it, and I'll argue that you shouldn't do it with your business.

In these situations, staff members end up making a mess that's actually more expensive to clean up than it is to do right the first time. Imagine being the professional heart surgeon selected to clean up the work of the "steady-handed" amateur—not a pretty sight.

Three Situations Where Outsourcing Makes Sense

There are three situations in particular where outsourcing makes sense. Rather than arbitrarily outsourcing these roles, however, it's useful to think about the decision in a systematic way. These three situations are as follows:

1. Your team lacks certain skills needed to reach your goals.

2. Your company lacks process expertise in a crucial area.

3. Your company has part-time needs that can't justify a full-time salary.

When you need specific skills and don't have them in-house, as in the first situation above, it's time to look externally. This is often the case when you lack not only particular skills internally, but also the technical knowledge to manage someone with such skills. In these situations, outsourcing, rather than hiring full-time, makes sense. The last thing you want is to have an employee whose performance you're not skilled enough to evaluate. It's better to outsource to a firm that addresses a broader problem, with consultants for whom the results are more intuitive and easier to understand.

For example, when sales go up for our clients, they know that our firm, as a whole, did a good job—and they will just trust us to manage our own keyword research team. If the same clients decided to hire their own keyword researcher, they probably would have no idea whether or not the keyword researcher did a good job. If sales stay the same, it's still entirely possible that the keyword researcher did everything right.

This leads us to our second situation: the lack of process expertise. It's one thing to have people with raw talents that are useful. It's another to have a process in place that can harness these raw talents. It's like saying a person with steady hands could be a great surgeon. While the raw physical skill is there, without a good process for making surgical decisions, the raw skill isn't effective. It takes both skills and process to get good outcomes. If you're missing one or both, it's best to outsource to a firm that has plenty of each.

In the final situation, outsourcing makes a lot of sense if you have only part-time needs and don't want to pay a full-time salary. If you need a keyword researcher or pay-per-click manager for only a few hours each week, why pay a full-time salary for each of those roles? It's better to outsource, because you get the competence of someone whose skills are being used—as opposed to part-time employees, whose skills become rusty from the lack of full-time use.

One real but not always obvious cost is the cost of staying current. This is a particularly good reason to rely on expert outside resources for Internet-related skills. Much of what you know now will be at best outdated, if not obsolete, within six months. It takes a full-time investment to keep current in order to be truly effective. If you're paying a a part-time salary to a part-time employee, who's paying the full-time investment to keep that employee current? It doesn't make sense for you to foot the entire bill, since you're only getting part of the benefit.

Realistically, nobody pays the bill, and you simply suffer by getting a part-time employee who does things that were effective two years ago but have since stopped working. Part-time employees can be a good option in industries where things don't change very quickly, but for Internet-related staffing, this option invariably leads to poor results.

Things to Look For in an Outsourcing Partner

If outsourcing makes sense for your situation, there are a few things to look for in making the right choice. This checklist will help you evaluate your outsourcing options and achieve the results you're seeking.

- Does the firm specialize in all types of eCommerce (impulse items, commodity goods, low-priced items) or in eCommerce specifically for high-priced products and services?

- Does the firm consider itself to be in the Internet marketing services business or the business of delivering more revenues and profits?

- Does the firm use a static methodology or does it continuously measure and improve everything it does, both internally and for clients?

- Does the firm base its decisions on opinions or on hard numerical facts?

- Does the firm hide how it does things or does it explain things openly so you can feel comfortable with what you're getting?

- Does the firm ask you what tasks you want done or does it ask you what outcome you want it to produce?

- Does the firm use a cookie-cutter, one-size-fits-all approach or does it develop a custom-tailored approach based on your company's unique assets and situation?

Outsourcing as an Expense Versus Outsourcing as an Investment

A colleague of mine once asked me, "What's the difference between an expense versus an investment?" My answer was simple: "Accountability." When you spend money on an expense, you never see anything in return. When you make an investment, you demand a benefit in return, and you hold people accountable if you don't.

I'm a big believer in accountability in all aspects of business. This philosophy comes in part from the fact that before my company evolved into a client service firm, we invested our own money on our own marketing campaigns. The system I've outlined in this book is the same system I've used when my own money is on the line.

Some would look at our methodology and characterize it as fanatically statistical. This comes from the fact that when my own money was on the line, I didn't believe in marketing expenses—only marketing investments. The only way to ensure the latter was to religiously track, analyze, and continuously improve every aspect of my marketing. Any process other than taking such a rigorous statistical approach meant I would be unable to hold my marketing dollars accountable—turning my marketing dollars into a wasted expense instead. Marketing should always be an accountable investment.

When it comes to looking for an outsourcing partner, I recommend using the same standard. When you've got the right firm, it should not feel as though you're spending money on it. It should clearly feel like you're making an investment in it. Any firm worth its salt should be able to deliver clearly measurable results within 90 days. If it doesn't, you should fire that firm. I stand by this—even if the firm in question were my own.

When it comes to outsourcing, think like an investor and you'll make much more effective choices.

CHAPTER 16

Big Ticket eCommerce Implementation Resources

In this final chapter, I'd like to introduce you to some useful resources. These resources will enable you to jump-start or refine your eCommerce efforts.

I'm constantly asked, "Bob, what services does your firm offer?" I'll start with a brief overview of the different ways we enable clients to grow their sales and profits faster using the Internet. I'll close the chapter by introducing you to one particular resource—the Big Ticket eCommerce Audit—that I strongly recommend if you're serious about increasing your big-ticket sales.

Our Service Offerings

We provide a range of services to support our clients in each phase of the Big Ticket eCommerce system. The services provided cover all the major steps of the system, including:

1. Strategy formulation

2.   Lead generation websites

3.   Traffic generation

4.   Ongoing analysis and optimization

Our company originally developed services around steps 3 and 4 of the Big Ticket eCommerce system—traffic generation and analysis and optimization. This is one of the primary reasons why so many of our clients have been able to double profits or sales from the Internet within 90 days of working with us.

In the early days, only five out of 10 clients achieved stellar results. The other half struggled. When we did an analysis of this situation, we discovered that the majority of the clients with poor results had one key thing in common: All of them instructed us to send traffic to their corporate brochure websites. So even though we were delivering website visitors, the visitors were not becoming leads. Although we pestered those clients to develop dedicated lead generation websites based on our proven experience, they often weren't able to create them (since it was such a big challenge for their staff) or they created them incorrectly.

To solve this problem, we launched our lead generation website creation service. This service was designed to make it easy for clients to quickly adopt a dedicated lead generation website. I hesitate to call this a website design service, because of the extensive statistical testing involved to create these sites. Instead of designing them from scratch, we work with clients to configure a handful of proven website elements—all of which are based on our extensive marketplace testing.

After making this change and insisting that clients use a dedicated lead generation website (instead of a corporate brochure website), we saw our track record improve—instead of five out of 10 clients doubling sales, eight out of 10 achieved these stellar results.

As much as we enjoyed such a good track record, we could not help but wonder what the heck happened to the two out of 10 clients for which things did not go so well. We analyzed these clients as well, and found that half of them had one major thing in common: While they used lead generation websites and received traffic and leads from our efforts, the leads were not turning into sales. Upon further investigation, we discovered that these clients thought of their Internet efforts as a stand-alone project—isolated from the rest of the company. They had a flawed strategy. The two most common problems were (1) a lack of clear financial objectives, and (2) a lack of integration between online efforts and the rest of the company's off-line business. When you don't have clear objectives, leads and traffic don't really matter. If you have a unique asset in your off-line business but don't incorporate it into your online efforts, it's hard to stand out and be unique among the prospects in your marketplace.

After getting involved in verifying and, in some cases, shaping a client's strategy, we found that our track record had improved from eight out of 10 clients achieving the desired success within 90 days to nine out of 10 clients achieving that status.

You might be wondering what happened to that one client out of 10 that didn't get the stellar results. Well, you weren't the only ones who wondered. We wondered too.

As you might have guessed, next we did an analysis of that. We found that in half of these cases, despite our best efforts, we were able to generate only 20% to 30% increases in profits within the first 90 days. In our world, we consider that a "failure"—though often the clients are still pretty happy. To date, we continue to work on figuring out what could be done better in these isolated cases.

In the other half of these imperfect cases, we found that we totally bombed—there had been no change in sales or profits whatsoever. When we looked carefully at these situations—which amount to just one out of 20 cases—we realized that these clients really never should have hired us to begin with. And after asking the clients some troubleshooting questions and learning more about their business, we realized in hindsight that we never should have taken them on as clients.

In our latest effort to make sure that we don't take on such clients—ones we know we can't help—we no longer automatically take on any client that wants to hire us. We evaluate the business and marketing plans of all prospective clients, to see if their situation is one that we can improve substantially. If there's a clear problem that's going to prevent the kind of results the client expects, we simply decline these no-win situations. Selfishly, we don't want to take on a client that would almost certainly tarnish our track record.

As part of this process, we now require all prospective clients to undergo a Big Ticket eCommerce Audit. Like the cardiac surgeon who won't see a new patient until after the patient has had a comprehensive physical, we now do the same. In a moment, I'll share with you how the audit works, why it benefits you enormously, and how you can take advantage of this "must use" resource.

The Big Ticket eCommerce Audit

The Big Ticket eCommerce Audit involves analyzing and evaluating your entire eCommerce effort—identifying the specific areas that, if improved, would increase sales and profits the most.

When you request an audit, you receive a detailed critique of your strategy, website, traffic, and analysis and optimization efforts. You'll see how you compare in these areas to other companies we evaluate.

Most important, you'll see the specific, often overlooked opportunities to improve sales and profits faster. We prioritize these opportunities and suggest the top few, on which we recommend you focus first. In some cases, these opportunities are internal to your organization—and we simply provide the outsider's objective, emotionally and politically uninvolved opinion. In other cases, the opportunities present situations in which one or more of our services would be an appropriate solution for you. In these cases, we outline the fees involved and let you make your own decision. Your company, of course, is under no obligation to contract with us, though we do credit your audit fee toward any of our services you may decide to use.

Finally, if during the course of the audit we discover that your situation is one of those no-win situations in which we don't think we can be of benefit to you, we will still complete the audit, but will refund your audit fee. We want every one of our clients to have an excellent return on investment when it comes to any of our services. If we don't feel our audit was productive given your situation, we'll proactively refund the fee. Similarly, if for any reason you did not feel the audit was productive and an immensely practical use of your time, simply let us know, and we'll refund the audit fee too. I like to think this guarantee is more than reasonable.

So the best-case scenario is that you request the audit and receive an analysis of what needs to be done to double your sales, profits, or other appropriate success metrics. The worst-case scenario is that you get an outside audit and expert second opinion on your Internet efforts, for free. Either way, you win.

If you'd like to request more information about this audit and, if appropriate, to schedule one, just email my office at **audit@bigticketecommerce.com** or call **877-349-2615**. Otherwise, I wish you the best of luck with your Big Ticket eCommerce efforts.

Printed in the United States
132632LV00013B/48/P